Operations Management

The Search for Effectiveness and Efficiency

John H. Van Vliet III

ISBN: 9781081689995

First Edition Second Printing

Published by

The Institute for Leadership, Business and Public Policy
Young Harris College
Young Harris, Georgia

John H. Van Vliet III, Ph.D.
1577 Victoria Woods Drive
Hiawassee, Georgia 30546
jhvanvliet@yhc.edu

DEDICATION

To Sami Van Vliet and to Jackie Van Vliet, two delightful
daughters who fill me with happiness and pride.

Table of Contents   page

Operations Management is a subset of general business management. This book begins with a brief summary of general business management concepts and then explores key elements of operations management.

Section One

Introductory Business Management

The Search for Effectiveness and Efficiency

Is our business doing well or poorly?

How well (or how poorly) is it doing?

What can be done to make things better?

Finding answers to questions such as these is the basis for the evolution of the study of business management. The study applies to "for profit" and to "not-for-profit" organizations. (The primary difference between "for-profit " and "not-for-profit" organizations is that all profits are retained in "not-for-profit" organizations while some profits can be distributed to owners and shareholders in "for-profit" organizations. Both types require good management.)

All businesses need to be concerned with **effectiveness** and **efficiency**. A business or a business process is effective if it can accomplish the assigned task. A business or process gains in efficiency when it can accomplish the assigned task with fewer resources. Resources include money (capital), labor, energy, transportation, raw materials, time, etc.

The effort to improve business has come to be divided into several distinct areas of study. Before examining significant some details of Operations Management, let's gain an overview of the following areas: **Strategy, Organization, Finance & Accounting, Operations, Sales & Marketing, HR, IT, Leadership, Decision-making, and Quality.**

Strategy

> What is the purpose of the company or organization?

> How does it propose to accomplish that purpose?

> How will it know if it succeeded or failed?

Most companies start with a relatively clear grip on the first two questions. Over time, they tend to lose sight of the answers. (The answer to the first question tends to degenerate into something like, "to make money", or "to help others.") Far too many companies never get a solid grip on the third question.

It is wise for managers to reflect on these three questions and to ensure they have good, clear answers to them. After that, it is wise to ensure those answers are understood by the other members of the organization.

Strategy plus Organization

An organization ought to start with a solid concept of what it intends to do. Why is it in existence? What are its goals? From there it is a logical step to ask how the organization expects to accomplish its goals. This is the organization's "strategy." A strategy should be clear and simple, even if it is not easy. As the organization plans how to execute its strategy, it will have to decide what people and resources it will require and how those people and resources should interact. This is called "organization." (Note that "organization" is used in two senses. In one case, "organization means a firm or business or agency, etc. In the other, it means the structure of that firm or business.)

It is vital for a business or firm to spend time ensuring it has a clear strategy and a compatible organization. These things tend to evolve or drift over time, so a wise manager will review them from time to time.

Finance & Accounting

This area covers several significant issues. The simplest "accounting" functions are to track outbound and inbound flows of money and to be able to know the "bank balance" situation of the company at any time. "Finance" has the task of dealing with capital formation and the management of money, credit, wealth and debt. A higher order function is called "managerial finance." That means using the cash flows, balances and indicators to evaluate the health of the company, to focus attention on areas that appear to be doing particularly well or particularly poorly, and to find the optimal instruments for holding cash, wealth, credit and debt.

Operations

The tasks of the Operations Manager or Operations section will be different from company to company. In general, however, the Operations Manager will be responsible for making things happen. Here is a list of responsibilities that typically land on the Ops Manager's plate:

Inside Sales (Taking orders initiated by customers –Using phone, fax, Internet, etc.)
Inventory Control
Warehouse Operations
Purchasing

Manufacturing/Assembling/Providing the Service
Packaging and Shipping
Information Technology (when not a separate function)
Quality
Training

So, if a function is not clearly part of Sales, Marketing, Finance, HR, Legal, or R&D, it usually winds up in Ops.

Ops places a premium on logic, structure, communication, leadership, and attention to important details. The company car is driving down the street towards its destination. Ops keeps the engine running and steers the car to keep it in the lane.

Sales & Marketing

Sales and Marketing are related functions that can be combined or handled separately. Both start with an assessment of the "market." (Who wants to buy our product or service? Who might want to buy it? Who else is providing the product or service?) The idea is to forecast the need for the product or service, to figure out where and to whom the product or service can be sold, and to anticipate how much of that product or service our company can expect to sell. (Forecasting is challenging. Science supports forecasting efforts, but forecasting remains more of an art than a science.)

Marketing deals with knowing the potential customers, their needs, their circumstances, and their preferences. Marketing goes well beyond advertising. Marketing starts with an analysis of the market by considering customers' locations and needs, the competition, and other factors such as laws and regulations. Marketing managers use the market analysis to allow them to consider the "Four P's" of Product, Price, Position, and Promotion. Advertising kicks in when we consider how to make our product or service attractive, and when we decide how to inform potential customers about what we have to offer.

Sales encompasses many activities. Sales often includes having a sales representative call on customers in order to help customers meet their needs using the products or services our company provides. At minimum, Sales includes a mechanism to receive orders from customers for the goods or service our company provides. The Sales function often also includes a "customer service" element.

Human Resources

Companies have to deal with multiple administrative tasks. The "human resources department" typically handles the regulatory and legal requirements associated with having employees. In addition, HR finds new employees, trains employees, helps to set pay and benefit scales, provides an avenue of complaint or redress, maintains personnel policies and procedures, maintains the paths for advancement and promotion, maintains disciplinary paths and records, etc. Sometimes the HR department also handles pay and benefits.

Information Technology

IT is an area that is growing in importance. IT includes everything from providing phones, common office computers and Email to running highly complex Enterprise Resource Planning (ERP) systems.

Information Technology is fascinating. Unfortunately, that means it can get out of control. From a business perspective, we probably do not want to be out on the "bleeding edge" of fascinating technological advancement. We want to remember that we are using the flow of information or the flow of commands and controls in order to accomplish clearly stated goals. The "Information Age" has created extraordinary opportunities, but it has also created pitfalls. Our IT department is to help us enjoy the benefits while avoiding the pitfalls.

Leadership

Leadership is a seemingly simple skill. It means defining and communicating what the organization is to do and inspiring the people to do it. Of course, that is actually quite hard to accomplish. There is much art involved in being an effective leader, and there is a substantial amount of "science" as well. It is an area full of ideas, theories and studies. I will offer you just a few simple leadership rules that might help you.

> Define the goal as clearly and simply as you can.

> Communicate it frequently.

>Take the tough jobs yourself. Lead from the front.

> Be honest. Never lie. Your followers may excuse you for making errors, but they will never trust you again once you lie to them or trick them.

> Accent the positive. Compliment good work and strong effort. Correct poor or ineffective effort. Punishment and harsh criticism merely discourage poor behavior. Praise encourages behavior and effort that go beyond the minimum. Besides, people enjoy working in a positive environment.

Decision making

Decisions get made, or not, one way or another. Outcomes fall somewhere on the continuum between good outcomes and poor outcomes. The goal of good decision making is to increase the probability of enjoying a beneficial outcome. Many theorists recognize the huge advantage one could gain by making even a marginal improvement in the quality of decision making. Accordingly, there are many theories about how we can improve our decision making styles and approaches. Please do not try to chase the latest decision making fads. Instead, look at each new theory you encounter and adopt what seems valuable to you. Look at the outcomes of your decisions. Evaluate the quality of your decision making. Learn from your mistakes and learn from your successes.

It is also important to recognize types of decisions. Some decisions are small, (of little consequence), such as the decision about the type of file cabinet to purchase for one office. Other decisions, of course, can be major, such as the decision about where to build a new facility. Obviously, we want to spend our precious attention units and time on the significant decisions.

Decisions can deal with "one-off" (one time) situations, or they can be deal with systemic or repeated matters. One-off situations simply require solutions that work. Situations that are likely to be repeated merit additional attention. The chosen solution for a repeating situation must not only work, it must work in a way that will permit it to be converted into a normal business practice that can be taught to the staff and followed.

Finally, decision-making is an art. Yes, we can support our decision-making with good numbers-crunching and scientific analysis, but we always face some degree of uncertainty. (Some poor managers like to use that uncertainty as an excuse to avoid rigorous analysis. Better managers use the rigorous analysis and combine it with subjective assessments.) Because of the uncertainty, some of our decisions will have bad outcomes. We should plan on that. Once you have made a decision and are ready to implement it, ask yourself questions such as:

>How will I know the decision was a good one?
>How will I know if the implementation is working or not?
>What are my fallback options?
>What should trigger the use of a fallback option?

Quality

Quality is sometimes a part of Operations. Sometimes it is a separate organization. Quality used to mean checking products before they were sold to ensure the products meet the standards. Now quality usually means developing a system to prevent failures in the first place and to create conditions for "continuous improvement." You will hear about quality management systems such as TQM (total quality management) or "Six Sigma." These quality systems are designed to help a company efficiently provide what it promises to provide.

Language can sometimes create confusion, and it certainly does in the case of quality. "Quality" has a common meaning. It means something that is better or finer. "Quality" also has a specialized meaning in business jargon. In business jargon, "quality" means being within tolerances, meeting the standards, or compliance and assurance of compliance with defined systems. (Please note that the jargon is evolving, and "quality" will almost certainly pick up a few more meanings. That is the nature of jargon.)

A disposable tablecloth that is of low quality in common terms could well be considered of high quality in business jargon because it meets its specifications perfectly. A very fine, precisely made, specialized brass fitting would typically be described as being "high-quality" in ordinary language, but it might be considered a quality failure in business terms because the manufacturing process took two extra days.

Quality is concerned with both effectiveness and efficiency. A production, assembly or service function must first be tested to see if its outcomes meets the standard (effectiveness). Then quality processes seek to find ways improve the efficiency of the function by maintain the level of effectiveness while employing fewer resources such as time, money and materials (efficiency).

Most quality processes recognize the value that can be gained by involving the whole staff in the search for improvement. Excellent ideas are often generated from within through the use of "quality circles" or other mechanisms to ask employees to look for ways to generate improvements.

Section Two

Operations Management – Key Topics

Section One above shows how Operations Management is one of several major areas in the field of business management. Now let's take a deeper look into Operations Management.

First, one must recognize operations management requirements will vary by each industry and by each individual business unit. We will consider concepts that generally apply across the board, but the concepts will have to be shaped and altered to fit particular situations.

We will look at the following key topics:

> **Typical Business Operational Structures**
> **Process Analysis**
> **Control**
> **Logistics and Supply Chain Management**
> **Inventory Management**
> **Quality Management.**

Chapter One: Business Operating Structures

Businesses organize themselves in a variety of ways and operate in a variety of ways. As a result, businesses create highly variable environments, and operations managers must adapt to those environments.

Businesses and organizations are often categorized as "For-Profit", "Not-For-Profit" or "Governmental". Businesses and organizations in any category must pursue effectiveness. (Is the business or organization accomplishing its purpose?) Most also pursue efficiency. (Accomplishing the purpose with the fewest resources.) The exception is government. Directors of government agencies virtually always seek to spend every dollar in their budgets as they anticipate no rewards for being frugal and they anticipate their ability to command higher budges in future years will be diminished if they demonstrate they can accomplish their tasks with less money than was budgeted. Therefore, government agencies are not really concerned with efficiency.

Another way to categorize businesses and organizations is by looking at the nature of what they do. Accordingly, we often see categories such as Manufacturer, Assembler, Distributor, Service Provider, Wholesaler, Retailer, etc.

Each business or organization, no matter its category, accomplishes its goals through a series of processes. (A process is a defined set of actions.) In their never-ending efforts to guarantee effectiveness and to improve efficiency, operations managers focus on these processes. Accordingly, it is sometimes seen to be useful to categorize business activities by the nature of the processes used. Common categories are:

Flow shop – Think of the classic assembly line. Many identical final products are made with each employee or machine performing a specialized and limited function toward the production of each final product.

Continuous flow operation – This is similar to a Flow Shop except the nature of the product is such that the transformation process cannot deal with individual components. Think of a sewage treatment plant or an oil refinery or the production of electricity.

Job shop – Each output is substantially different from any other output, (or the number of identical outputs is small before it is time to start making a different item.) Think of a custom home builder or a handy man.

Note that while these categories obviously evolved from the study of the production of items, they can be applied to services as well. For instance, a company that sells the service of inspecting and maintaining air conditioning systems might have characteristics of a job shop because each AC installation is particular. A hospital's in-processing might resemble a flow shop as the patient is seen in turn by a set of administrative and health specialists.

These categories are just somewhat useful ways to group business organizations and may help us think about what is happening on the operations side of the business. No matter what set of categories apply, operations managers will quickly start to focus on the steps or actions each person or machine is expected to perform as the organization accomplishes its goal. Being able to conduct a formal analysis of each significant process is a key ability operations managers must develop.

Chapter Two: Process Analysis

Process analysis is a nuts and bolts element of operations management. Assume we have designed a process (a set of actions) to make widgets that meet our standard for a widget. Can we make the process more efficient? If our company makes widgets, and someone can find a way to make 2% more widgets in the same amount of time for no extra cost, (or at a small cost relative to the value of the additional widgets), that is a very good thing. By the same token, if someone can modify our process to create widgets with fewer manhours or less energy or fewer materiel resources, that would also be a very good thing. Operations Managers must search for such efficiencies. Operations managers study the structure of operations (process analysis) to see if they can understand where there are underutilized resources, bottlenecks, etc. in order to improve the efficiency of the process.

There are multiple ways to make an item or to provide a service. While these ways are vividly illustrated in flow shop operations such as assembly lines, they exist, more or less well-defined, in the production of any item or in the provision of any service. There is a starting point or condition, a set of intermediate actions and a final point or condition. The set of intermediate actions constitutes a process.

A classic example of a process would be the production line where an item moves from point to point and workers, who have specialized in the demands of a particular step of the production, perform the same action on each succeeding item.

Operations managers want to analyze processes in order to find areas for improvement. Generally, the analysis requires one to identify discrete steps in the process and then measure the performance of each discrete step. Please note processes and circumstances vary widely. It is not possible to develop a detailed method suitable to analyze all processes. Instead, one must understand concepts, learn from simplified examples and then apply and adapt the concepts to whatever process is actually to be analyzed.

What is meant by "measuring the performance of each step"? That depends on the nature of the process and the circumstances. In general, we want to know how many items are processed at each step and how much time is spent in processing. In addition to time and production amounts, in some situations we might want to measure the amount of energy employed, the number of manhours of a particular type, the amount of a particular input, the amount of scrap, the number of failures or errors, etc.

Initially, let's look at the analysis of time and how much is produced. Let's imagine a church group has established a team to create boxes of disaster relief supplies to be sent and distributed to people who have been forced from their homes and who are staying at relief shelters.

Process Analysis Illustration

The church has gathered donations in a gym. There are tables set up along the center of the court. Teams of volunteers will start by placing an empty box at one end of the tables and then push the boxes through several steps until the boxes are sealed, marked, and stacked for delivery.

Assume the person in charge has already planned the actions required, prepared the location, organized the teams, and issued instructions. (Note: This is not a trivial assumption.) Let's analyze the process as it is being performed.

We start with a person who is assembling boxes and placing completed boxes at the end of the first table. For the sake of common terminology convention in this book, I will identify this initial activity as STEP ONE, and note it includes one STATION with one OPERATOR (or EMPLOYEE, PERSON, VOLUNTEER, etc.)

[Note that a process is a set of interconnected steps. Each step may have one or more stations. This is the convention used in this book, but the terminology elsewhere may change depending on the circumstances of the process. Focus on the ideas. Don't become too rigid about jargon.]

As we observe the process in action, we note the operator was able to place six assembled boxes on the table in one minute. This measured observation translates into two key process analysis elements. The first is CYCLE TIME, the time required to complete one unit of analysis. The second is CAPACITY, the number or volume of output in a given time.

CYCLE TIME, Step One: In this case, the unit of analysis is "boxes", and the operation completed six boxes in one minute. Depending on our time preference in the process analysis, we can say the CYCLE TIME for Step One is:

10 seconds per box

or some fraction of another unit of time

CAPACITY, Step One: The step was observed to require 10 seconds to prepare a box. That translates into a CAPACITY for Step One of:

6 boxes per minute or 360 boxes per hour

or some other output based on a different unit of time.

The box is pushed on to STEP TWO where a single operator adds a blanket to the box and pushes the box to the next person. Observation shows the OPERATOR at the single STATION in STEP TWO spends 12 seconds completing the task.

CYCLE TIME of Step Two is 12 seconds per box.

CAPACITY of Step Two is 5 boxes per minute.

In STEP THREE we find one OPERATOR on one side of the table, and another OPERATOR on the opposite side of the table. Each OPERATOR has a box and places sets of food items in the box. Each OPERATOR can complete a box in 30 seconds. Thus, STEP THREE has two STATONS, each with its own operator. Together, the stations finish two boxes every 30 seconds.

CYCLE TIME of Step Three is 15 seconds per box. (… from 2 boxes in 30 seconds)

CAPACITY of Step Three is four boxes per minute.

In STEP FOUR a single OPERATOR at the first STATION in STEP FOUR spends 5 seconds placing a jacket or sweater in the box and pushes the box to the next STATION where the same OPERATOR spends 7 seconds placing an item of clothing in the box and marking the box as Man, Woman, Girl or Boy. Accordingly, the STEP has two STATIONS, one requiring 5 seconds and the next requiring 7 seconds, but only a single OPERATOR. Accordingly, the CYCLE TIME for the step is 5 seconds plus 7 seconds.

CYCLE TIME of Step Four is 12 seconds per box.

CAPACITY of Step Four is 5 boxes per minute.

In STEP FIVE, a single OPERATOR at the single STATION spends 10 seconds adding packing material and sealing the box and moving the box to the end point.

CYCLE TIME of Step Five is 10 seconds per box.

CAPACITY of Step Five is 6 boxes per minute.

The next page has a sketch of the Relief Box process. Sketches are commonly used to visualize a process.

(There is no standard format for such sketches. Do what makes sense in the situation.)

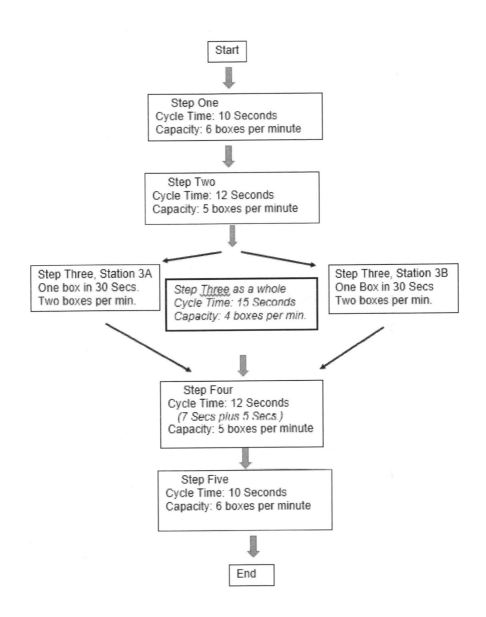

Start

Step One
Cycle Time: 10 Seconds
Capacity: 6 boxes per minute

Step Two
Cycle Time: 12 Seconds
Capacity: 5 boxes per minute

Step Three, Station 3A
One box in 30 Secs.
Two boxes per min.

Step Three as a whole
Cycle Time: 15 Seconds
Capacity: 4 boxes per min.

Step Three, Station 3B
One Box in 30 Secs
Two boxes per min.

Step Four
Cycle Time: 12 Seconds
(7 Secs plus 5 Secs.)
Capacity: 5 boxes per minute

Step Five
Cycle Time: 10 Seconds
Capacity: 6 boxes per minute

End

Capacity of the Process: Let's investigate the capacity of the process as a whole. We see the lowest capacity is 4 boxes per minute at step three. That capacity restricts the capacity of the process as a whole to just 4 boxes per minute. (The other steps have larger capacities, but that doesn't change the fact that only 4 boxes per minute can pass through step three.) We say step three is the BOTTLENECK as it sets the limit on the capacity of the process as a whole. Note in this case there was only one bottleneck, but it is possible to have several steps in a process all operating at the lowest capacity and all constituting BOTTLENECKS.

Promotion of the next bottleneck: Recognize that improving the capacity of a bottleneck often means some other step in the process becomes the next bottleneck. (In our Relief Box example, if we were to improve the capacity of step three to 5 ½ boxes per minute, the capacity of the process as a whole would then be 5 boxes per minute because of the new bottlenecks at steps two and four.)

 SLACK: What about the steps in the Relief Box example that have capacities in excess of 4 boxes per minute? Those steps have capacity beyond what is needed to operate at the process's limit of 4 boxes per minute. We say those steps have SLACK. Step one can complete four boxes in just 40 seconds. There are 20 seconds of SLACK per minute available at step one. Step two has 12 seconds of SLACK per minute. Step three is a BOTTLENECK. It has zero SLACK. Step four has 12 seconds of SLACK per minute and Step five has 20 seconds of SLACK per minute.

(Note in some cases is it convenient to think of SLACK in terms of units of output rather than units of time. For instance, one could say step one can produce two more boxes beyond the required four boxes per minute for the process as a whole. As is always the case, analysists should be flexible and approach each particular process on its own terms.)

Process Improvement – The Search for Efficiency

Once the analysis is finished, one will have identified the capacity of the process as a whole along with any bottlenecks and slack. The total cost or amounts of the inputs can be divided by the capacity to arrive at a measure of resource productivity. For instance, the Relief Box process requires 6 people and produces 4 boxes per minute (or 240 boxes per hour.) Six people working for one hour is 6 manhours. 240 boxes divided by 6 means the productivity is 40 boxes per manhour. (One can measure all other resources in a similar fashion, and one could convert all resources into money in order to arrive at a cost per box as a measure of the efficiency of the entire process.)

We would like to improve the efficiency of the process. One of the ways to do that would be to figure out how to increase the capacity of the process as a whole at a cost that makes sense. We start by looking at bottlenecks. What can be done to improve the capacity of the bottleneck(s)?

Let's go back to our Relief Box sample process. We see the operators in Steps one and five each have 20 seconds of slack per minute. Might it be possible to alter the tasks to improve the total capacity by creating a third station in step 3 and manning that station part of the time with operators from step one and step five splitting their time between their primary step and step 3? The math tells us we might be able to do that. However, be careful about real world considerations. Is there sufficient space? Would the flow be disrupted as operators move back and forth? Would confusion surface?

Another way to search for efficiency is to study the actions at the bottlenecks. For instance, suppose we see that the operators in step three are walking to stacks of food to collect the items needed for the boxes. Could repositioning the stacks of food reduce the travel time? (Thereby cutting the cycle time and improving the capacity.) Perhaps the operator at step 5 could assist step 3 by periodically placing food items in shopping carts close to the boxing stations. That might reduce the cycle time at step 3.

Sometimes shifting resources will not generate all of the possible improvement or enough improvement. Sometimes one needs simply to add resources to the bottleneck. That works if the costs are outweighed by the gains. In our Relief Box example, imagine we simply add a station and operator to step three. The extra station means the cycle time at Step three is 30 seconds per box per station divided by three stations or 10 seconds a box. The capacity of step three would now be 6 boxes per minute, so steps two and five, the new bottlenecks, set the capacity of the process as a whole to 5 boxes per minute. At five boxes per minute, the process is generating 300 boxes an hour using 7 manhours. That means the productivity per manhour is 42.8 boxes, which is higher than the 40 boxes per manhour of the original process.

One has to look at each situation in order to devise workable ways to increase the capacity of bottlenecks.

Other Efficiency Factors: In addition to seeking increases in capacity, operations managers can also seek efficiency in other ways. Can personnel in slack steps finish their work early and do something useful with their slack time? Would the substitution of less expensive resources work just as well? Are there ways to reduce waste while maintaining production levels? Could we usefully automate certain steps? Would it be cost efficient to adopt better, stronger or faster tools? Would training certain people improve performance? Etc.

As a caution, note that times and counts may vary. Measured times might be averages, or only applicable with fully skilled operators. Defects might diminish outputs. Machines might break. Power might fail. People might make mistakes. Variation increases even more when we are analyzing processes generating services rather than products. Accordingly, do not assume processes can consistently perform at the designed output. It is also useful to build mechanisms to "surge" beyond normal capacity should it become necessary to make up for shortfalls.

Buffers, Charge Time and Discharge Time

Buffer inventory: Buffer inventory, also called "Work in progress", is the collection of partially finished items that are waiting their turn to be processed by the next step. Look at what can happen in the Relief Box example if operators at steps one and two work at their full capacity. The operator at step one will push 6 boxes a minute to step two. The operator at step two can only finish 5 boxes a minute, so one box each minute will build up between steps one and two. The same thing happens between steps two and three. Note there will be no buffers built beyond step three as steps four and five are fully capable of handling the boxes leaving step three at its rate of four boxes each minute.

Buffer inventory can be useful because it provides a place for partially finished work to be parked while waiting the attention of the next step. Buffers can prevent "blocks" caused by a lack of a place to pass on completed work or "starvation", stalls caused because no work is ready to be processed. Properly planned buffers can also create the possibility of releasing an operator for other purposes. In the Relief Box example, the process as a whole has a capacity of 4 boxes per minute or 240 boxes per hour. In an 8 hour day, the process will generate 1920 boxes. Note that step one is capable of handling 6 boxes a minute so step one could, if there is sufficient room for buffer inventory, prepare 1920 boxes in only 340 minutes (5 hours and 40 minutes), freeing the operator for 2 hours and 20 minutes of useful work elsewhere. (Similar calculations shows 1 hour and 10 minutes of time savings are possible at Step Two.)

The process analysis we have covered so far applies to processes in normal operation. However, sometimes it is critical to consider what happens if a process starts fresh with no "work in progress" already integrated into the process. ("Work in progress" refers to the set of partially completed items to be found within the steps of the process and within any buffers.)

Let's go back to our Relief Box process and imagine what things look like just as the church group is ready to begin. The items are gathered, the workers are ready, and the tables are empty. As the operator of step one starts assembling a box, there is nothing for anyone else to do. Let's follow the first box. After 10 seconds have passed, the first box will move to step two where the operator there will spend 12 seconds selecting, folding and adding the blanket. Then the box goes to one of the stations in step three where the operator will spend 30 seconds adding food. At step four the operator will spend 5 seconds at the first station adding clothing and 7 seconds at the second station marking the box. Finally, the operator at step five will spend 10 seconds packing and sealing the box. Whew! The first box was completed 74 seconds after it started at time zero. Seventy four seconds is the time required for any one box to move from start to finish. Note the first box reached step five 64 seconds after the process started. At that point, (64 seconds after the start), the process was "fully charged". That is to say each operator at each station is no longer waiting to begin, but instead, the operator is functioning as he or she would be functioning during normal operation. We can say the "charge time" is 64 seconds.

The charge time is the time required to move a process from an empty start to a normal functioning level.

What happens at the end of the day? Perhaps, if there are plenty of boxes worth of material to be packaged, we can simply stop and leave partially finished boxes (the "work in progress") at each step and come back the next day to pick up where we left off. However, sometimes it is important to clear the line of all work in progress. In our example, when the operator at step one starts to assemble the last box of the day (and we assume all operators were content to operate at the rate of four boxes per minute, thus not building any "buffer' inventory"), then 74 seconds will be required to see that last box reach the end point.. The "discharge time is 74 seconds. Please note the discharge time would be longer if all of the "work in progress" in buffer inventory is also to be discharged.

The discharge time is the time required to empty a process from a normal function level.

Charge and discharge time can be critically important in processes such as food preparation or processes requiring material to be maintained at high temperatures as these processes must halted to be cleaned from time to time.

We have covered sufficient basic concepts of process analysis to permit the study of virtually any process. Because processes and circumstances are different, the analyst must flexibly adapt the concepts to fit the situation.

A Short Presentation of Process Analysis Terms

Imagine a two step widget manufacturing assembly arrangement.

Step A: (one station) (45 seconds per widget)

Step B: (three stations) (Two minutes per widget at each station)

The **cycle time** for a station at Step A is 45 seconds.

The **capacity** for Step A (measured per hour in this case) is 80 widgets per hour. It is the capacity of the single station. (Remember that capacity can be measured per week or month or whatever.)

(60 min per hr. TIMES 60 sec per min) DIVIDED BY 45 sec per widget = 80 widgets/hr.

The **cycle time** for a station at Step B is 120 seconds. (Consistent units of measure)

The **cycle time** for Step B as a whole is 40 seconds. It is the capacity of a single station divided by the number of stations in the step.

The **capacity** at Step B (measured per hour) is 90 widgets per hour. It is the capacity of the single station TIMES the number of stations

30 widgets/hr. per station times 3 stations = 90 widgets per hour.

Alternatively, the capacity of Step B can be determined using the cycle time for Step B as a whole. (60 min per hr. TIMES 60 sec per min) DIVIDED BY 40 sec per widget = 90 widgets/hr.

Step A is the **Bottleneck.** It is the step with the lowest capacity. It limits the capacity of the operation as a whole to 80 widgets per hour.

Step B is **Slack.** It has excess capacity. It is capable of producing 90 widgets per hour, but the bottleneck at Step A means it only has to produce at 80 widgets per hour.

Chapter Three: Control

In the previous section, we learned about processes and process analysis. We are now able to identify the cycle time of a step in the process, the capacity of each step in the process, bottlenecks in the entire process, the capacity of the entire process and the location of slack in any of the steps.

Process analysis helps us design a new process or evaluate an existing process.

Please remember, the first requirement of a process is that it be EFFECTIVE. (That is, it will do what is required.) The next step is to seek EFFICIENCY by finding ways to accomplish the required tasks with fewer resources.

Please also note that process analysis applies to processes using things as well as processes performing services.

But once a process seems to be well designed so that it is both effective and efficient, there remains the concern that the process might not actually be working as designed. Accordingly, operations managers seek to employ techniques to "measure the pulse" of processes. Are the process working as designed, or not?

Operations managers can be sure that people on the receiving end of the product process or service process will be quite unhappy if the process fails. (This is analogous to driving a car down the street. You will certainly know it when you drive off the road. Your "process" for driving will have failed vividly.) Of course, it would be better to detect problems and looming failures before the process fails.

(Hmm… the car is drifting to the right of the lane. I should make an adjustment before I run off the road.) Evaluating the performance of a process is called "Process Control" or "Process Monitoring and Control"

Process monitoring and control consists of deliberate steps to check on the "health" (the correctness or accuracy) of the process plus deliberate steps to correct situations that fail (or are about to fail) to meet the standard.

Controlling processes requires these systematic steps:

- Setting performance standards
- Measurement of actual performance
- Reporting or communicating results
- Comparing actual performance with standards
- Analysis of deviations
- Taking corrective action
- Confirming corrective action succeeded

Ideally, measuring actual performance and comparing results with standards should be simple, immediate and automatic with a positive actions or signals to identify failures or movement toward failure. The most robust control systems add automatic responses to correct deviations from the standard.

In its simplest and least efficient form, process control might be nothing more than conducting a final inspection of the end result of the process. Items or outcomes that fail to meet the specifications are scrapped or discarded. This form of final check to assure the product or service meets defined specifications might be necessary for high risk situations such as the manufacture of parts used in nuclear reactors or the maintenance processes for aircraft engines. However, running a final "quality assurance" inspection on everything would be quite expensive. In addition, a final check only tells you if the process as a whole is working or not. It does not provide information about what step in the process might be failing. We can avoid wasting a lot of time and other resources if we can spot problems quickly and early in the process. Therefore, we would like to do better than merely having a final quality assurance inspection.

In order to design a good monitoring and control system, we should start by examining the process to decide what should be observed and measured as the process is being utilized. Obviously, it would be inefficient and nearly impossible to observe and to measure every action, so we should probably look for critical points. Then we want to figure out the easiest effective way to see if the results at the critical points are as expected and required. Because situations and processes are so variable, it is not sensible to try to create "one-size-fits-all" control mechanisms. Instead, operations managers should consider the circumstances and design or improve monitoring and control systems as needed.

Here are some characteristics of a good process monitoring and control system:

➢ The system should be cost effective.
➢ The system should be simple to operate and to maintain.
➢ The system should be responsive. (It should report problems quickly.)
➢ Measurements should be sufficiently precise, but not overly precise. (If the standard is to be within a meter, we do not need to measure to the nearest millimeter. A less precise instrument will do.)
➢ The system often includes automatic corrective responses to deviations from the standard performance levels.
➢ The system should provide useful data and reports.
➢ The system should send a signal if the system itself goes out of order.
➢ The system and its installation should be well-documented. (This helps us look for problems that may arise in the monitoring and control system rather than the process itself.)

Chapter Four: Logistics and Supply Chain Management

Logistics

Logistics is a term used to describe the many activities associated with managing the flow of things to required places in order to meet the needs of the organization and its clients. Supply Chain management and inventory management are subsets of logistics.

Supply Chain Management

Operations managers use process analysis as one of the key tools for managing the activities under the direct control of an organization. However, outside factors can also have a profound effect on the performance of an organization. Supply Chain Management covers some of the concepts operations managers can use to deal with external factors.

What is a supply chain? Visualize all of the things that had to happen to permit a homeowner to use a nail to hang a picture on the wall. Iron ore had to be mined and transported and used to make steel. Then the steel had to be taken to a factory to make the nails. The nails were packaged and sent to a wholesaler who sold them to a retailer who sold them to the homeowner. This description is actually a simplification of reality, and it ignores all sorts of other factors such as machines, power, communication, administration, finance, etc. Still, the idea is clear. Lots of people are involved in many ways to provide even something as simple as a nail.

Happily, a supply chain manager doesn't have to deal with every detail from raw material to final consumer. Instead, supply chain managers typically only look one or two steps "upstream" or "downstream" from their own organization. Imagine a company that makes cars. The company assembles cars from parts and materials that it manufactures itself or that it purchases from suppliers or vendors. (This is the "upstream" direction.) It uses distributors to sell the cars to consumers. (This is the "downstream" direction.)

Here is a simple sketch to show how a manager in a manufacturing firm might visualize the firm's supply chain:

Basic Supply Chain

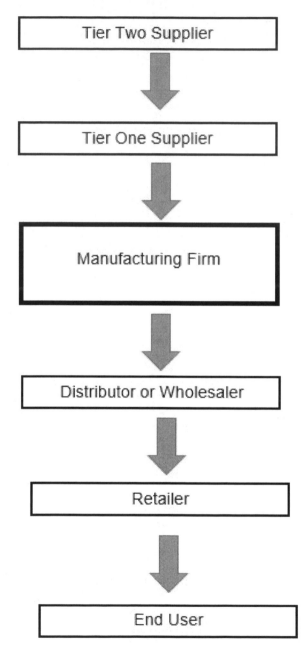

Tier Two Supplier

↓

Tier One Supplier

↓

Manufacturing Firm

↓

Distributor or Wholesaler

↓

Retailer

↓

End User

From the manufacturer's point of view, the firm purchases goods and services from Tier One suppliers. Those Tier One suppliers, of course, must purchase goods and services from other suppliers who are described as Tier Two suppliers from the perspective of the manufacturing firm. Similarly, a manufacturer often sells to wholesalers who sell to retailers who sell to end users.

This very simplified view can alter based on the situations, but the principles remain the same.

A supply chain manager in the manufacturing firm is aware that the success of the manufacturing firm depends on smooth and efficient functioning by all parts in the supply chain. A failure by a tier two supplier could be felt by the manufacturer and even by the end user. Accordingly, the supply chain managers (at any level) will seek to understand and monitor the situations at key members of the applicable supply chain.

The paragraph above introduced the concept of "key members" of a supply chain. By extension, some members of the supply chain will not be key members. Categorizing a supply chain member can be done by asking how easy or hard it would be to cope with a disruption or failure by the supply chain member. For instance, our manufacturing firm might outsource its janitorial activities to a tier one janitorial service. While a failure would be vexing, it would not have a significant impact on output or quality, and it would be simple enough to hire a competing service. Accordingly, the tier one janitorial service would not be key. Conversely, consider a tier one supplier that provides a specialized bracket used in the assembly of the final product. Such a tier one supplier would by key and merit close attention from the supply chain manager at the manufacturing firm.

What kind of "attention" should a supply chain manager devote to key suppliers or key downstream firms such as wholesalers and retailers? The answer is based on effectiveness and efficiency as well as profitability.

From the point of view of "Effectiveness", the supply chain manager wants to maintain the required rate of flow of parts, supplies, products and services from upstream members of the supply chain and also provide the required rate of flow of products and services to downstream members. Close liaison with a focus on meeting commitments is essential. (Building reaction plans in the event of failures will also be helpful.) At a minimum, a supply chain manager will probably keep an eye on inventory levels and the quality of key parts and supplies maintained by tier one suppliers.

From the point of view of "Efficiency", the supply chain manager will seek to identify and to eliminate unnecessary activities and costs or seek to find ways to accomplish necessary activities at reduced cost. (Can less expensive packaging be used? Can shipping schedules be adjusted to be more convenient and/or less expensive? Is there a smarter way to handle counting or reporting or other administrative matters? Are the specifications for parts and services over-stated? Etc.)

Profitability is, naturally, another key area of focus. Unless a firm owns all the major elements of the supply chain, there is a natural competitiveness built into the relationships between members of the supply chain. After all, the purchase price of the final product or service is almost always set by a competitive market, so the profit in a sale will be determined by the sum of the costs of the sold item or service. It is very natural to squabble over the shares of profit earned by each step in the supply chain.

I would like to share some wisdom I gained from Bill Simon, then the Sales Manager for McNaughton-McKay of South Carolina, a distributor of electric parts and automation services. One of Bill's customers was rebuilding a production line and, given the sizes of the expected orders, was seeking price reductions on automation equipment. Bill hosted a meeting with the customer, the distributor (Bill) and the manufacturer of the bulk of the needed equipment. Bill got the meeting off to a great start by noting that whatever agreement they reached had to be a "win-win-win". The customer had to be getting needed equipment on time and at an acceptable price. The distributor had to be earning an acceptable profit, and the manufacturer had to be earning an acceptable profit. By focusing on the search for the "win-win-win" rather than by setting up a competition among the three, Bill created a positive environment where the three participants focused on ways to get the business done at lower cost rather than fussing about price points. They wound up with a streamlined set of deliveries and expectations which squeezed costs from the deal and permitted the manufacturer and the distributor to enjoy almost normal profit margins while the customer benefitted from a price reduction.

Another example of supply chain management in practice comes from an experience with Ford Motor Company. Ford opened up bidding among distributors to determine which distributor would be the normal Tier One source for electric parts. The twist that Ford added was the distributor was not only to bid a low initial price point, but the distributor was also to commit to price REDUCTIONS in the following several years. To the astonishment of the distributors, Ford claimed the distributors should still earn the same amount of profits or even greater profits in future years even at the reduced prices. How could that be? Ford's practice was to generate a meaningful partnership with its Tier One suppliers. Ford would send efficiency experts to the suppliers to identify places where unnecessary costs could be eliminated. The cost savings could come from any portion of the supplier's operation even though the first focus would be on studying the flow of parts to Ford. Savings can often be found in less costly scheduling of deliveries, simplification of administration, ordering, billing and payment, alteration of packaging, reduction of errors, etc. Both Ford and the Tier One suppliers were open to altering practices to reduce costs.

While it is useful to work with other members of the supply chain, it is also important to plan for the unexpected or for trouble. Supply chain managers need to have alternatives in mind in case of a breakdown in the supply chain. Sometimes that means giving up the expected advantages of sole-sourcing arrangements and deliberately accepting some inefficiencies by maintaining business relationships with two or more competing sources. The supply chain manager has to balance higher costs against the insurance of having alternative sources in place.

Supply chain managers also deal with the questions of out-sourcing, sole-sourcing, and off-shoring.

Out-sourcing is the opposite of in-house production or performance. Many actions, including administrative actions and actions that are part of the direct production of goods and services, are performed directly by company employees. Some actions, however, are better done by specialist firms that are not part of the company. Out-sourcing is typical for certain support functions such as grounds maintenance, janitorial services, communication services, provision of energy, etc. Out-sourcing may also be used to provide critical parts or services that are difficult or expensive to provide in-house. Generally speaking, a supply chain manager will recommend out-sourcing in circumstances where the outside firm can reliably provide the proper quality and number of desired goods and services at lower costs. Conversely, supply chain managers will generally prefer to maintain direct, in-house control of the provision of goods and services that determine the reputation and success of the company.

Sole-sourcing, obviously means choosing to have a single source of supply. The anticipated advantage is the ability to build strong ties with the supplier in order to gain loyalty, good (but perhaps not the lowest) pricing, and confidence in the quality of the provided goods or services. A sole-sourcing situation gives up the expected advantages of constant competition among suppliers, although the competition and the benefits of competition or expected to be gained during the period of bidding for a sole-source agreement.

Off-shoring applies when the goods and services in the supply chain are provided by tier one or tier two suppliers based in foreign countries. Such suppliers may offer better prices or better access, and sometimes it may be that there is no domestic option anyway. However, off-shoring carries with it all of the complications of international business, including tax, legal, transportation, communication, foreign exchange rate fluctuation, and international affairs complications.

In a nutshell, the supply chain manager maintains strong communication, awareness and relationships with actual and potential partners up and down the supply chain in the steady effort to maintain effectiveness and quality while improving efficiency.

Chapter Five: Inventory Management

While supply chain management focuses mostly on factors external to the organization, inventory management adds special attention on the stocks of parts, material and supplies used within the firm. "Inventory" is a term that applies to many aspects of an organization's operation. A manufacturing company will have an inventory of finished goods, an inventory of work in progress, an inventory of components, parts and materials used in the manufacturing process, an inventory of spare parts and repair equipment, an inventory of test equipment, and inventory of office supplies, etc.

All of those inventories represent money tied up in the effort to produce and sell goods and services.

http://pdsinventory.com/

The task of controlling inventory levels is typically performed by people called inventory managers or purchasers or warehouse managers or office managers.

Inventory Management Basics

1. Inventory costs money, so we do not want to have excess inventory.

2. Stockouts cost money and wreck performance, so we do not want to run out of required inventory.

3. Inventory Management implies finding the most effective and efficient way to keep inventory costs down while still having enough inventory when we need it.

Key Terms

Cost of Holding or Holding Cost – A dollar value to represent the cost associated with keeping items on hand. Typical costs are insurance, provision for loss or deterioration, cost of counting and maintaining items, and interest costs on borrowed money. Sometimes companies add a portion of capital costs and utility costs. The holding cost is generally defined as a percentage of the purchase cost of an item. (See Appendix C for a discussion of the difficulty of selecting proper values for the Cost of Holding.)

Cost of Ordering or Ordering Cost – A dollar amount to indicate the cost of placing an order, processing the receipt of the order, receiving, inspecting and storing the items, and paying for the order. (See Appendix C for a discussion of the difficulty of selecting proper values for the Cost of Ordering.)

Dead Stock – items no longer being used or sold. The usage rate is zero over a certain period of time, and there is no expectation of future need.

Lead time – The expected time between placing an order for an item and receiving the item.

Order Point (sometimes called "Reorder Point") – The level of quantity available that triggers the need to order more. Typically, the order point is Usage Rate times Lead Time plus an additional amount of Safety Stock. Be careful with time units of measure.

Order Point - (time based) – Sometimes organizations place orders on a calendar basis, so the order point would be a date rather than a quantity.

Order Quantity – The amount of an item that is ordered.

Quantity on Hand – The amount of an item present (in the stockroom or warehouse or shelves, etc.).

Quantity Available – The Quantity on Hand less committed items… (such as items that have been sold to a customer but not yet picked for delivery.)   CAUTION – frequently people say or write Quantity on Hand when they really mean Quantity Available. The context should clarify the matter.

Quantity On Order – The quantity that has been ordered but not yet received

Reorder Point (See "Order Point")

Safety Stock (or Buffer Stock) – an amount of an item that is held in inventory as insurance against unexpected delays in delivery or abnormal increases in usage or any other unanticipated problem. Think of it as insurance against a stockout.

Stockout – running out of a needed item. (See Appendix A for thoughts about the cost of stockouts.)

Usage rate – The quantity used over a period of time. (Be careful to pick a useful unit of measure for time and quantity.)

The sketch below shows an idealized view of how inventory management might work. We can see the level of units in stock steadily decreases over time. If nothing is done to order more units, we will run out of stock. To avoid running out of stock, we set an "order point", a stock level that triggers an order for more units. Notice the ordered units do not arrive instantly, so we calculate the expected "lead time" for the new units to arrive and ensure our order point is high enough to meet our expected usage during the lead time. Notice we also have an amount of "safety stock" included in our order point value. Given that the real world has variation, we need the safety stock to protect us from stockouts due to variations. The vertical line shows the level of stock rising by the order quantity when the order is received.

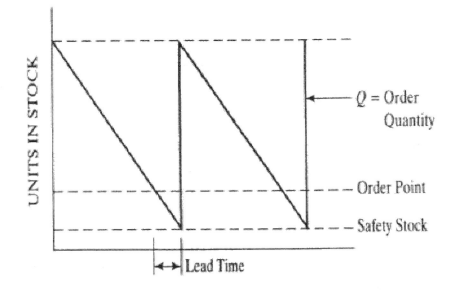

Of course, in the real world, usage rates will not be quite so regular, so the sketch below suggests what one might see in actual practice.

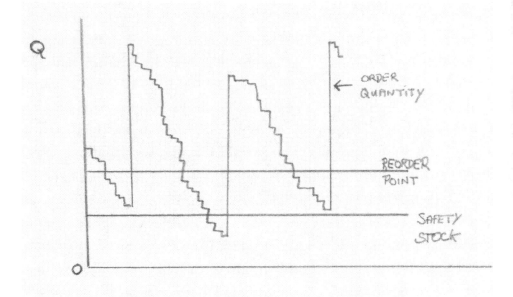

"When to order". "Safety Stock" and "How much to order"

Inventory managers must cope with a critical tension between two competing goals. In order to maximize effectiveness, inventory levels must be large enough to avoid the disruption caused by stockouts. In order to maximize efficiency, inventory levels must be as small as possible. This awkward tension is managed by paying careful attention to the key questions of "when to order",

"How much safety stock is required" and "how much new stock should be ordered". We will study each of these key questions. (In general, these three elements are often referred to as "inventory controls".)

When to Order: When should you place an order?

Most commonly, the need to place another order for an item is triggered by the inventory level. (Quantity on hand is frequently used, but Quantity available is more precise.) The inventory level that triggers the need to place an order is called the "Reorder Point" or the "Order Point".

The reorder point commonly is the sum of two inventory amounts. The first inventory amount is found by multiplying the usage rate for the item by the amount of time required to receive the order, (the Lead time). The second inventory amount is the safety stock or buffer stock. Therefore, the formula for the common reorder point is:

Reorder Point = (Usage rate x Lead time) plus Safety Stock

Sometimes the time to place an order is determined by the calendar. For instance, one might place an order at the end of the month or the start of a season.   In this situation, the purchaser must set adequate Safety Stocks to protect against stockouts caused by variable usage patterns in between the scheduled time to place orders.

Note that purchasers may sometimes delay placing orders in order to collect sufficiently large orders to qualify for "deals" offered by suppliers or shippers. Once again, the purchaser has to evaluate the levels of safety stock in order to permit some delays in placing an order.

Safety Stock: Safety stock is insurance against a stockout. Shipments can be delayed. Orders can be misunderstood or incorrectly filled. Usage patterns can vary. The safety stock is extra stock on hand (or available) to permit the company to deal with the unexpected. Figuring out how big a safety stock should be requires consideration of how critical the inventory might be, how quickly one could fill an emergency order for the inventory, how expensive the inventory is, how erratic the usage patterns are, etc. A common rule of thumb for safety stock levels is to set the safety stock as the multiple of lead time and usage rate. (This level of safety stock allows a routine response to a failed shipment.)

How much to Order:

There are multiple approaches to setting the Order Quantity, (how much to order). Some of them also include methods to set the Reorder Point. Several methods are introduced below:

One of the first (and worst) methods I encountered might be called the **"Eye Ball Method"** or "**Walking the Shelves."** An inventory manager explained it and demonstrated it to me. He said he just "walks the warehouse shelves" to "eyeball" the amounts of inventory and writes down what he thinks should be ordered. The thought behind the method is that an experienced manager should be able to use his gut instincts to know what stock levels are required. I handed the manager a pad of paper and asked him to "walk" one row of inventory shelves and write down the inventory he would purchase. Then I took his choices back to the office and checked the sales history on the items he wanted to buy. In some cases, he appeared to have made a good choice as the quantity on hand only amounted to about two weeks to four weeks of usage, and he was suggesting an order quantity of several weeks or several months of usage. However, these "good purchase" conditions only applied to a little more than a third of the items on his list. Another third of his choices would be adding stock when the existing stock levels exceeded 10 months of usage; a grossly inefficient choice. About a sixth of his choices would be adding stock which was desperately needed (and the purchase was far too late) as the quantity on hand was at zero or less than a week's usage. Grotesquely, another sixth of the choices would be adding stock to inventory items on hand that were "dead"… the items hadn't moved in over a year.

I was able to show that inventory manager the inefficient and ineffective flaws in the Eye Ball Method, and train that inventory manager to adopt a more efficient system. You should be aware of the system only because it is still in use. Should you encounter it, converting to any other system will lead to improvements in effectiveness and efficiency.

In the **Min-Max** inventory system, the inventory manager sets a level of inventory (the "Min" or minimum) which will trigger the need to reorder. (This "min" value includes safety stock considerations as well as usage amounts during time required for delivery.) The amount to order is determined by the "Max" level. One orders enough to bring the inventory level back up to maximum.

This system is simple to use and works well with automated systems. It requires careful thought in the establishment of the initial "min-max" levels (and in the periodic resetting of those levels.) However, once the levels are established, the purchasing can be done automatically or executed by a clerk who requires only minimal skills or knowledge.

In the **ABC Classification** system, the inventory manager divides the inventory into three classes. "A items" are most critical or valuable and typically make up 20% of the inventory. "B items" might be the next 30% of the inventory. "C items" might be the least important or least valuable items and make up 50% of the inventory.

Here is an example of how one might structure reorder points, safety stock and reorder quantities using the ABC Classification system:

Class A items have a reorder point of one week's usage plus one week's usage as safety stock. The order quantity is one week's usage.

Class B items have a reorder point of one week's usage plus two week's usage as safety stock. The order quantity is two week's usage.

Class C items have a reorder point of one week's usage plus two or three week's usage as safety stock. The order quantity is three week's usage.

(Note: This example assumes ordered items can be delivered in a week or less. It also assumes usage rates are not very erratic.)

This is a rather unsophisticated system, but it is simple and helps to focus a purchaser's attention on the most critical items. The "A' items will have to be ordered most frequently, so purchasers will have to pay more attention to them.

In the **classification system**, the inventory manager ranks the inventory based on the value of inventory that moves through the warehouse. The dollar amount controlled by each item is calculated by multiplying the annual usage times the cost of the item. The items are rank-ordered and divided into 13 categories or "classes". Items with zero usage (at the bottom of the list) fall into the Dead Stock classification. The rest of the items fill classes 1 through 12 with each classification level having one twelfth of the value. The Class One items (at the top of the list) would a relatively small number of items whose product of usage times cost is large. The Class 12 items (the last items in the list of active stock) would be composed of a large number of items whose low costs and/or low usage rates mean each item only contributes a small amount to the total value of the inventory that moves through the warehouse in a year.

All items in the classification system typically use a reorder point equal to the sum of the safety stock plus the product of usage rate times lead time.

The interesting variation is in the determination of order quantity. The order quantity for Class One items is one month's usage. Class Two items have two month's usage as an order quantity, and so on until Class Twelve which has 12 month's usage as the order quantity. (Dead Stock, Class 13, obviously has zero as an order quantity.) The effect of this method is to direct the purchaser's attention proportionally to those items that carry the largest value of inventory through the warehouse. Items with lower classification numbers will have to be ordered more often during the year than items with higher classification numbers. The assumption is that time spent fine-tuning the situation with Class One items, for instance, is more useful to the company than time spent with Class Ten items, for example.

See Appendix B for a suggestion that inventory managers could increase their value to the company by focusing on returns not just on proper inventory controls.

EOQ (Economic Order Quantity)

Given the development of strong business management software systems, systems that rapidly and easily keep track of usage, orders, deliveries, prices, costs, quantities on hand, quantities on order, lead times, etc., many organizations have embraced Economic Order Quantity as the most efficient way to establish an order quantity. It is in common use for a good reason, and I encourage its use. (See Appendix C for a discussion of the difficulty of selecting proper values for the Cost of Ordering and the Cost of Holding, two values used in EOQ.)

Consider a situation using TESTCORP Incorporated, a company that uses widgets in the manufacture of its finished products and orders those widgets from an outside supplier. The inventory manager has developed a system to determine when a new order should be placed, and his system has triggered the need to order more widgets. If he orders too many widgets, the cost of keeping them in inventory (insurance, property taxes, maintaining and counting the widgets, the cost of the capital used to buy the widgets, etc.) will be too high. If he orders too few widgets, he will have to order them again very soon, which means the company will have to pay the cost of ordering widgets (time spent placing the order, the cost of receiving the order, certain shipping costs and other costs) too frequently. Accordingly, the purchasing manager would like to balance the costs of ordering against the cost of holding inventory. The Economic Ordering Quantity (EOQ) method identifies the proper balance and establishes an ideal order quantity for the widgets.

EOQ uses three values to calculate the most efficient quantity to order. Those three values are usage, U, the cost of placing an order, Co, and the cost of holding inventory, Ch. Each company has to decide the proper values for Co and Ch. (It is hard to calculate these two values with precision. Companies gather what information they can and then rely on the "art" and experience of the inventory manager and the company finance officer to determine the values that will be used. (See Appendix C.) TESTCORP Inc. has decided to use $47 as Co and 8% as the annual holding cost factor.

The EOQ equation is quite simple. The EOQ is the square root of the product of twice annual usage times ordering cost divided by holding cost.

EOQ $= \sqrt{2*U * Co/Ch}$

Caution: We have to ensure the units of measure are consistent. If holding cost, Ch, is measured in dollars per year per item, then usage must be measured in items per year and ordering cost must be measured in dollars. (One could use weeks and Japanese Yen, but the units must be consistent.)

If widgets cost $20 each, then the inventory manager calculates the holding cost to be $1.60 per widget per year (8% of $20). If TESTCORP Inc. uses 400 widgets per year, the EOQ is $\sqrt{800 * 47/1.6}$ or 154 widgets, (rounding up.

In an ideal world, TESTCORP would order 154 widgets each time its inventory of widgets was reduced to the level that triggered a new order. (Notice that TESTCORP Inc. will not necessarily order exactly 400 widgets in a given calendar year. Inventory carries over from one year to the next.)

However, the world is rarely ideal. There may be some additional constraints or factors that have to be considered when placing the order for widgets. Perhaps the standard packaging for widgets is ten to a box. The purchaser at TESTCORP Inc. would probably order 16 boxes, (160 widgets). Perhaps there is some special price reduction for orders of a certain size, or a shipping cost reduction for orders of a certain size. The purchaser might adjust his order quantity of widgets to take advantage of those benefits if they are significant. The point is that EOQ offers an ideal order quantity for the order, but other constraints or opportunities might cause a company to deviate from the recommended quantity. It is fine to deviate provided the person placing the order is aware he has deviated and can show that the deviation makes sense.

EPQ (Economic Production Quantity)

Inventory managers and operations managers must consider a slightly different situation when the company produces some parts or items in-house rather than ordering them from a tier one supplier. In that situation, EOQ is not quite ideal. Here is an explanation:

Let's move forward a few years from the situation above used to describe EOQ. TESTCORP Inc. has altered its operations. Now, instead of buying widgets from an outside source, TESTCORP Inc. produces its own widgets in-house. This changes many things. One of the things that changed is TESTCORP no longer places an outside order for widgets. Instead, it has to instruct its own team to make a certain number of widgets at a certain time. That means the cost of ordering, Co, no longer applies. In its place, there is another set of costs. These are the costs associated with giving instructions and setting up production. We call these costs "set up costs" or Cs. If tooling is involved, these costs can sometimes be quite steep. Using the same type of logic as for Economic Order Quantity, one can now seek an ideal number of widgets to produce in-house. This is called the Economic Production Quantity.

As annual holding costs and usage rates have not changed, there is a strong temptation just to substitute Cs for Co in the EOQ formula. That temptation is not too bad. In fact, it is a good start. The first part of the EPQ formula is exactly that.

$$EPQ = \sqrt{2*U * Cs/Ch} \quad \text{... (more)}$$

However, the simple substitution of the setup cost for the ordering cost is not sufficient. Here is why:

If TESTCORP were to order 154 widgets from a tier one supplier, as it would in an EOQ situation, all 154 would arrive at once, and inventory levels would jump. The situation is not quite the same when TESTCORP is making widgets in-house. Widgets are produced over time, and they are also being consumed over time. The average inventory levels will be lower in a production situation than in a situation where the items are ordered. We need to consider the reduced average inventory levels by adding another factor to the formula. That factor is composed of two rates. One rate is the production rate, P. The other rate is the usage rate, U. These rates can be in items per year, items per week, boxes per hour or any other rate so long as both rates use consistent units of measure. The EPQ formula turns out to be:

$$\text{EPQ} = \sqrt{2{*}U {*} Cs/Ch} \; {*} \; \sqrt{P/(P - U)}$$

MAJOR CAUTION! The formula uses usage, U, twice, but the usage might be expressed with different units of measure in each radical. See the example below.

Let's see how this works for TESTCORP Inc.

TESTCORP still requires 400 widgets each year. Its holding costs are still 8%. Because of in-house production, each widget now costs $19 to make instead of $20 to buy. Holding cost, Ch, is now $1.52 (8% of $19) per widget in average inventory per year. The time and materials needed to set up the machines to makes widgets cost $55 per batch, so Cs is $55. The machines can make one widget in 20 minutes, so the production rate, P, is 3 widgets per hour. TESTCO uses 400 widgets each year. We need to convert that from a yearly usage rate to an hourly usage rate. Because TESTCORP operates 14 hours a day five days a week for 50 weeks per year, the usage rate, U, is 400 widgets per year or 0.114 widgets per hour (400 widgets per year/3500 hours per year).

We will use the annual usage rate in the first part of the equation, but we must use the hourly usage to match the hourly production rate in the second part of the equation.

One can now calculate EPQ.

$$EPQ = \sqrt{2 {*} U {*} Cs/Ch} \ {*} \ \sqrt{P/(P-U)}$$

$\sqrt{800 * 55/1.52} \ * \sqrt{3/ (3\text{-}0.114)} = 174$ widgets (rounded up)

(If widgets are packaged in units of 10 as part of the production process, TESTCORP would use a production batch size of 180.)

(Did you notice that U has two different values in the two parts of the equation? It would be nice to differentiate the symbols, but such a convention has not yet taken root, so you must be alert to the situation.)

Conclusion: EOQ is used to calculate an ideal ordering quantity for items ordered from a supplier. EPQ is used to calculate an ideal batch run for items manufactured in-house. In each case, the ideal value comes from balancing the cost of holding inventory against the costs needed to place an order or start production. In each case, additional constraints might cause a manager to deviate from the ideal (least expensive) order quantity.

"The Bag" Method

The inventory management methods we discussed so far, (with the exception of the unfortunate "Eye ball" method), are suitable for large inventories supported by information management systems and computers. However, sometimes the situation calls for a simple, or even primitive, solution. For example, consider the need to maintain stocks of toner and staples for an office copier machine. Perhaps an administrative assistant in the office is tasked with keeping the copier properly supplied. Yet, the administrative assistant is focused on other matters and lacks the time to conduct frequent checks on the supply of toner and staples. The office routine would be disrupted, and its functioning would be diminished if the copier were to need toner, but all of the replacement cartridges had been used. ("Oh No! We need toner but we are out of stock!") This sort of situation is perfect for "The Bag" method of handling inventory. It works like this:

The administrative assistant stashes a toner cartridge and a box of copier staples in a bag or box in a closet or drawer. Then the administrative assistant tapes a note in the place where stocks of toner and staples are normally kept. The signed note says, "Come see me if you need toner or staples".

Typically, someone will use the last cartridge and say nothing at all. When the next person sees only a note instead of a toner cartridge, that person will ask the administrative assistant for a cartridge and the copier will be put right. The need to pull a cartridge from its stash (its "bag") will trigger the need to reorder more toner. When the new toner arrives, one cartridge goes back into "the bag" and the others are placed in the normal supply point.

The beauty of this method is that it is simple, it prevents the bad effects of a stock out, and it is easy to administer.

The concept of "the bag" method can be applied in multiple situations. An ideal example surfaced when a customer agreed to buy all of its electric parts from McNaughton-McKay, a distributor of electric parts and automation services. As a condition of the sole-source arrangement, the customer provided a list of critical parts to McNaughton-McKay and demanded a commitment that the parts on the list be available any time the customer should need to place an order for them. The sales team happily agreed and then passed the requirement to the operations manager to implement. Well, wait a minute, how in the world could the inventory management system be structured to reserve a quantity of parts just for that special customer? How could one avoid the possibility of another customer's order consuming all of the stock of a particular part just a minute before the special customer placed its order? It was a nightmare.   The solution was to pull a set of the guaranteed items and put them in a special box in a special location in the warehouse. Then the operations manager added a note to that customer's account that would print on any back order form triggered by a stockout for that customer. The note said: "Contact the operations manager who can fill this order right away." Of course, should an item ever have to be taken from the special box, it would have to be replenished as soon as possible. The system worked well. For the cost of tying up a small set of guaranteed parts, McNaughton-McKay was able confidently to guarantee the availability of those parts, thus keeping a good customer fully satisfied. (For those of you who have some knowledge of computerized inventory management systems, you will know that the items in the special box would have to be coded in a way to maintain track of the items without making them available for general sale. The method for doing something like that will vary from system to system.)

Inventory Management Deviations – The Human Touch

The common systems for inventory management generate suggested answers to the "when to order" and "how much to order" questions. However, purchasers and inventory managers are not robots, and experienced purchasers and managers will sometimes deviate from the suggested reorder points and order quantities.

One of the obvious deviations will concern <u>standard packaging levels</u>. If an item is typically sold in dozens, and the EOQ system calls for the order of 117 of the item, the purchaser of manager should actually order ten dozen (120). Rounding up or rounding down is a matter of judgment, but generally, one rounds up.

Sometimes tier one suppliers (vendors) may offer special deals for purchases that reach certain dollar amounts. In such situations, a purchaser or manager might look ahead to anticipate the next required purchases of items from that vendor in order to add sufficient items to the total order to take advantage of the "deal". Again, judgement is required.

Shipping adds costs to the flow of inventory. In some situations, purchasers or managers can alter the timing of orders (and associated quantities) in order to combine shipments and reduce shipping costs. "Drop shipments", items ordered from a vendor to be delivered directly to a customer, can also be attractive ways to cut costs. Once again, judgement and awareness of the particular situation are required.

Unusual orders: Sometimes a customer will have a strange situation and want to order an unusually large number of an item. (For instance, the customer might be planning an expansion.) Filling such an order from normal stock can boost the risk of stockouts for the customers who are part of the normal usage pattern for that item. A wise inventory manager will try to fill such unusual orders with a special "drop shipment" or a special stock replenishment order rather than from normal stock.

Covering shortfalls or problems: The real world is imperfect. Orders can be incorrect for a variety of reasons. Shipments can be delayed or lost or damaged for a variety of reasons. Purchasers or inventory managers need good relationships with shippers and tier one suppliers in order to solve problems. It is prudent to have up-front agreements about how to expedite shipments of orders, (to include using faster but more expensive shipping methods, such as "next-day air".) It is also prudent to be aware of local sources of items in the event of emergency. Sometimes it might be clever just to pay retail price from a competitor's stock rather than to disappoint a customer with a stockout.

VMI - Vendor Managed Inventory

Vendor Managed Inventory, VMI, is a relatively new development. It stems from vendors being frustrated with clients who were frequently having to demand expedited deliveries or clients who frequently returned items. Some of those vendors were convinced they could do a better job of managing the clients' inventory, so they offered to do just that. Here is an example:

Panduit sells channel for electrical cables and wires. Panduit was a tier one supplier for McNaughton-McKay and believed it could manage the relationship so both Panduit and McNaughton-McKay experienced lower costs and the end using customers experienced fewer sockouts. Panduit proposed a pilot test of its VMI system to prove it would work. Panduit was granted access to inventory data and sales data of Panduit products at one of McNaughton-McKay's branches. Panduit used an EOQ-type of system plus its own system for setting reorder points to decide when and how much to deliver to the McNaughton-McKay branch. Panduit also instructed the branch to return items Panduit judged to be excess. Panduit earned its normal payment for its items and intended to pay the cost of managing the inventory from cost savings. At the end of a year, the pilot program was judged to be a grand success. The cost of Panduit inventory tied up in McNaughton-McKay's warehouse was virtually the same as at the start of the year, but total sales were actually higher. Stockouts were greatly reduced, and returns were controlled. The Panduit VMI pilot program saved money and improved performance for McNaughton-McKay while cutting costs for Panduit as well. Both companies enjoyed improved profits.

VMI will not always work well, but an inventory manager would be wise to utilize VMI in those cases where a vendor can demonstrate the ability to manage its portion of the inventory with greater effectiveness and efficiency.

Keeping Track of your Inventory - - Counting

Inventory levels can be incorrect because of data entry errors, physical losses, theft, etc. Inaccurate inventory levels can lead to multiple problems. Counting the inventory is done to discover errors and to bring recorded inventory levels into line with actual inventory levels. Counting also help to identify items that are misplaced or deteriorating.

The "sheet-to-shelf" method of counting provides a list of items and expected quantities to the person doing the counting. The "shelf-to-sheet" method provides a list of locations to the person who is counting. The person then must report what and how much was found at each location. The sheet-to-shelf method is less accurate as the person who is counting is predisposed to see on the shelf what the sheet told him or her to expect. Scanners and barcode readers add accuracy and reduce the time required during counting.

A full inventory (often requiring a business to shut down during the period of the inventory) has the advantage of achieving the most accurate count right after the completed inventory. As the accuracy fades over time, the accuracy will be at its lowest (and most problematic) level just prior to the start of the next full inventory. Cycle counting is a technique to count a portion of the inventory each day.

The frequency for counting a particular item can be based on its value, its usage, its attractiveness to thieves, its tendency to be poorly counted, etc. Generally, the inventory control system will identify items to be counted and checked. The warehouse team might count during lulls in other business, or it might count at the end or start of the business day. As a rule, each item should be cycle counted at least once during the year. In this system, the level of inaccuracy should stay roughly constant over the year

Chapter Six: Quality Management

Language can sometimes create confusion, and it certainly does in the case of quality. "Quality" has a common meaning. It means something that is better or finer. "Quality" also has a specialized meaning in business jargon. In the business sense, "quality" means being within tolerances, meeting the standards, or compliance and assurance of compliance with defined systems. (Please note that the jargon is evolving, and "quality" will almost certainly pick up a few more meanings. That is the nature of jargon.)

Some people become tangled up with the meaning of "quality". A disposable tablecloth that is of low quality in common terms could well be considered of high quality in business jargon because the tablecloth meets its specifications perfectly. A very fine, precisely made, specialized brass fitting might be considered a quality failure in business terms because the manufacturing process took two extra days.

Given that "quality" in the business sense means the product or service meets the specifications or standards, it is natural to expect the first focus of business quality systems will be on "effectiveness". Accordingly, business quality systems will first want to contribute to making certain the business is producing goods or services that meet the standards. While that is, indeed, the first task of a quality system, it is also natural to employ the quality system to contribute to the goal of "efficiency". Accordingly, the quality system will also seek to reduce the costs associated with meeting the standards. All business quality systems should be judged by those two goals, and operations managers should assess their quality systems according to those goals.

There are multiple quality systems in use by businesses and organizations. The following sections will present some common elements found in typical systems. Then we will introduce a few of the commonly used business quality systems

Quality Methods or Approaches

A. **Quality Control** – Focus on Output

Consumers or customers are obviously disappointed if the product (or service) does not perform correctly. In order to avoid selling defective products, companies sometimes resort of full inspection of each finished item. Alternatively, companies may resort to statistical sampling of finished products. Full inspection is more certain than sampling, but it is also more expensive. Both full inspection and statistical sampling fail to detect causes of defects and also fail to detect defective products early in the production process so as to avoid adding work to an already defective piece.

Full quality control inspections of products prior to their release for sale or use was one of the early responses to the need to ensure an organization's products meet the stated standard. This level of quality control is still practiced in some organizations and for certain types of products. Components of spacecraft, aircraft, and critical installations are often treated with rigorous final inspections.

B. **Quality Management or Quality Assurance** - Focus
   on Process

 Rather than simply checking finished products, Quality
Management or Quality Assurance systems study the
production processes in order to identify root causes of
failures and eliminate them. These quality systems not
only seek to eliminate the causes of defects, (thereby
assuring the final products will meet the standards), they
also seek ways to accomplish correct results at lower
costs.

There are many quality management systems such as
TQM, ISO 9000 (or other numbers), Lean and Six Sigma.
They will be introduced below.

Quality management systems generally start by carefully
defining expected actions and results. Then they apply
well-defined measurements throughout the process to
identify points of failure or deviation from the standard.
They incorporate the experience and focus of employees
to help identify root causes of problems and to discover
areas for possible improvement. (A common term for
groups of employees is "quality circles".) Record
keeping, analysis of data, creativity and proper follow-up
are key components of an effective quality system.

C. Quality of Service – Focus on service rather than products

Seeking to achieve proper quality in the production of things isn't enough. We also need to seek quality in the delivery of services. A common problem with the delivery of services is the awkwardness of identifying sound measurements. Quality systems dealing with services are, frankly, still maturing.

Current Quality Systems

In this section, we will introduce five commonly used quality systems.

TQM – Total Quality Management, TQM, was one of the first quality management systems to embrace quality assurance rather than quality control. Unlike many modern software-based quality management systems, TQM emphasizes key concepts that any organization should embrace as it seeks to build processes that will consistently delivery effectiveness and efficiency.

TQM has a special "customer" focus. Not only does it recognize the typically understood customer, the person or company that purchases the organization's product or service, TQM also puts emphasis on the "internal customer", the next person or stage in a process. People performing any step in a process are required to know and understand the requirements of the relevant internal customer as well as the typical end user who will buy the product or service.

TQM's scope is broad and total. Quality is not just a matter for a quality control team or even just the manufacturing or assembly teams. Instead, all members of the organization, receptionist, purchaser, book-keeper, mail clerk, Information Technology staff, etc. are involved in the continuous effort to maintain effectiveness and to improve efficiency. An organization's actions are seen as sets of integrated and inter-related processes which are to be studied, measured, and continuously evaluated and improved.

Quality circles, teams of people from who perform an identified function in a process plus people from the previous and subsequent steps in the process, are empowered to seek continuous improvement. Decisions are to be fact-based, fully communicated, rapidly executed and quickly evaluated.

ISO – The International Organization for Standardization (International Standardization Organization) is a group headquartered in Geneva, Switzerland. It publishes thousands of standards applicable to hundreds of industries. The following example shows how ISO works:

BMW is an ISO-certified maker of automobiles. As part of their ISO certification requirements, companies must take steps to ensure the quality of parts and materials purchased from tier one suppliers. The ISO standard permits companies to accept without question parts and materials purchased from ISO-certified suppliers. If a supplier is not ISO-certified, then the company must engage in a significant and repetitive set of inspections to assure parts from the non-"ISO-certified" source meet proper standards. A tier one supplier seeking to do business with BMW was asked by the purchasing manager at BMW if the supplier was "certified under ISO-9001". (ISO-9001 is one of the ISO common standards.) The reply was "No, but we have an excellent quality management system different from ISO-9001". The supplier was told to try again after it had been ISO-certified. The ISO standard, in effect, pressures companies to use tier one suppliers who are also ISO-certified.

The supplier's operations manager, eager to have BMW as a customer, set about gaining ISO certification. A study of the ISO-9001 standard showed it contains explicit rules about the structure and organization of a quality management system, but all of the actual specifications for products and actions are left undefined. In effect, ISO-9001 defines rules about the quality system but lets the certified organization develop any specifications for the standards of its products or services and for the standards of its internal processes. Once an organization has built a quality system, it would call in a certifying agency to inspect its system. If the system conforms to the ISO standard, then the organization will be granted a certificate and can legitimately become part of the community of ISO-certified organizations. (The certificate is renewed with periodic re-inspections.)

The operations manager visited an ISO-certified company to learn about the certification process. It quickly became clear the certifying agency necessarily will know very little about the actual business being certified. Instead, the certifying agency will be fully immersed in the administrative demands of the ISO standard. In effect, the certifying agency seeks answers to two questions. First, does the quality system conform to the administrative specifications in the ISO standard? Second, if the quality system defines an action or task that is to be done, was the action actually taken or was the task actually performed? The operations manager assimilated the rules of the ISO standard and followed the standard as a "cook book" to ensure the quality system would pass the certification inspection

It quickly became clear that the goal of earning ISO certification is not necessarily linked to the goal of building a robust quality system. In fact, if the goal is the most pain-free certification, then it would be prudent to build the most stream-lined and simple system that will touch all of the bases required for certification. That becomes the "formal" quality system that will be inspected and certified. Other quality matters, particularly any that might invite questions from the certifying agency, could be omitted.

Here is a small example of the silliness that can be generated by a certifying inspector who focuses on compliance rather than quality. McNaughton-McKay sells cable by the foot from large spools of cables. It uses a simple machine that causes a rotating wheel to measure lengths of cable drawn through the machine. As part of the quality process, McNaughton-McKay wanted to ensure the machine was properly calibrated, so each morning a test length of twenty five feet of cable would be drawn through the machine to confirm a reading of twenty five feet. The certifying inspector reasonably asked to know how the twenty five foot test length had been measured initially, but he was not satisfied with the answer that it had been measured using a tape measure. He wanted to know if the tape measure was properly certified or calibrated. Given that a common hardware store tape measure is accurate to within a tenth of an inch for every thirty feet, and given that the McNaughton-McKay standard was to sell cable to the nearest foot, the operations manager argued a common tape measure was quite sufficient. The certifying inspector shrugged and pointed to the standard requiring any calibration to be performed using fully certified measuring devices. Strict compliance with the written standard forced the operations manager to order a more expensive certified tape measure or face denial of ISO certification.

Setting aside some of the bureaucratic silliness that ISO certification can generate, one should ask if the ISO quality standards work well or not. The answer has to be, "It depends". The ISO standards do a good job of defining structures and elements that would be valuable components of a strong quality system. An organization can incorporate those elements and structures into a robust quality system that is compliant without having too many bureaucratic components. The onus is on the designer of each particular quality system to build a system that contributes toward effectiveness and efficiency while still meeting the ISO standard.

Because ISO rewards companies whose tier one suppliers are ISO-certified, ISO creates a collection of companies with a vested interest in encouraging other companies to use ISO as well. Accordingly, ISO has a large footprint among companies, and moving away from ISO is difficult even if a different quality approach seems more suitable.

Companies which use ISO as their quality standard should examine every ISO requirement against the specific demands of their circumstances. Use the useful portions of the ISO standard to help craft and maintain a strong quality system. Comply with the less useful portions of the standard in a minimal way in order to become or remain certified. Avoid adding anything to the quality system that would complicate certification.

LEAN- LEAN Manufacturing, LEAN production and Toyota Production System are terms that define a set of approaches and concepts associated with improving operational results. Hence, LEAN practices are explicitly or implicitly associated with quality management systems.

LEAN starts with a deliberate definition and study of "value". Value is that combination of price and performance sought by the organization's customers.

One then examines the "value stream", which is the set of processes and actions used to create the product. The purpose of examining the value stream is to identify and to eliminate actions that do not add value. "Flow" is the next factor to be studied. The idea is to remove irregularities and to create a flow that is smooth and efficient. "Pull" is a powerful concept in LEAN. Pull requires managers to switch their thinking from "pushing product to the next step" and to think instead of serving the next step by sensing the requirements or needs of the next step. (The next step's requirements "pull" items from the preceding step.) Finally, LEAN seeks "perfection", that is across-the-board efforts to make things better by finding and eliminating waste, smoothing functioning, and adding value more efficiently. (Note the search for perfection covers everything from administration to production to shipping, etc.)

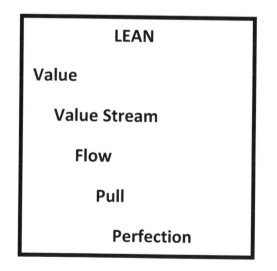

LEAN's concentration on value and its focus on eliminating waste is exceptionally attractive. "Of course", one might say. "That makes sense for any business." Well, yes, it does, but it is very common for business practices and actions to take on lives of their own and to drift from the natural idea that all actions are to add value. LEAN's deliberate focus on value and waste helps to correct that tendency and keep effectiveness and efficiency firmly in mind.

Six Sigma- Six Sigma is a popular approach to seeking ever greater accuracy in the performance of processes. The name comes from the use of "sigma" in statistics to represent one standard deviation. If a process is so accurate that the distance between an upper tolerance limit and a lower tolerance limit could contain six of the process's standard deviations, then errors or failures would be exceedingly rare. Thus, the use of "Six Sigma" to name the approach emphasizes its powerful focus on measured and confirmed accuracy.

Every action in a set of processes has a result. That result is either acceptable or not. In any step of a process, unacceptable results, (called errors, defects, failures or faults), reduce effectiveness and efficiency. Six Sigma offers concentrated and well-focused methods to root out unacceptable results in every step of every process in a business.

The acronym DMAIC helps people understand Six Sigma.

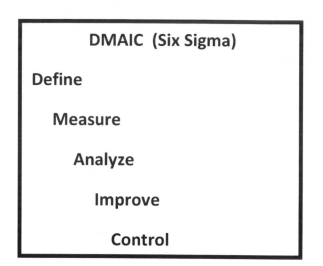

At each step in a process, practitioners of Six Sigma perform the following actions:

"Define" means to be totally clear about what is to be done and the standard to be used to know that something was correctly accomplished. One starts with the big picture by addressing the broad task to be accomplished and the standards to be attainted. One then maps out all inter-related processes.

"Measure" means to identify each point at which data should be gathered along with a clear understanding of how that data is to be acquired and how much confidence one should have in the accuracy of the data.

"Analyze" means to turn the data into information. What does the data tell us? Are the process's results within tolerance levels or not? If not, why not? What are the root causes of out-of-tolerance deviations from the standard?

"Improve" means to address root causes for deviations. What could be down to alter circumstances so the root causes of errors are eliminated (or reduced)? One then must plan and implement the corrective actions followed by testing to ensure the corrective actions work.

"Control" means to put in place a system to detect and correct any drifting of the process from its designed state. Is the process working as designed? How do we know? If the system is drifting or failing, what steps (automatic or otherwise) are to be taken?

As you can see, DMAIC, highlights Six Sigma's vigorous emphasis on data in its search for near perfection. Practitioners of Six Sigma concentrate their attention on:

> What needs to be known?

> How one is to know it? (Measurements and systems of measurements)

> What is to be learned from data? (Root causes of defects)

> What is to be done to address root causes of defects?

> Is the process working as designed?

> How does one know the system is working correctly or not?

A small caution needs to be raised concerning Six-Sigma. The fascination with achieving near-perfection in all parts of a process could lead to improper investment decisions. For example, consider a situation in which a machine produces one defect in every ten items. Such a failure rate is certainly not going to match the Six-Sigma standard. Suppose a root cause analysis indicates the machine should be redesigned in order dramatically to reduce the failure rate and meet the Six Sigma standard. The projected cost of the redesign effort plus installation would be such that the improvement would cost twenty five cents for each avoided defect. Alternatively, suppose the failed parts can be detected, rejected and recycled at a cost of fifteen cents each. (The fifteen cents includes the cost of fabricating the failed part, installing a testing and sorting mechanism and recycling the defects.)

The cost effective solution is to test and reject failures rather than to adopt the more expensive solution of redesigning the machine. Yet, a practitioner whose focus is only on finding that golden Six-Sigma outcome at each step might opt to redesign the machine. Should you encounter something like this, broaden the scope a bit. Consider the original machine plus the testing and sorting addition as a single step in order to satisfy the purists. (It is also proper to keep looking at possible solutions for that original machine. Can a more cost-effective redesign be found? Might it be sensible to schedule buying the redesigned machine when the existing machine reaches the end of its life expectancy?)

Six-Sigma Belts: No discussion of Six-Sigma would be complete without acknowledging the Six-Sigma Belt certification levels. Six-Sigma's approach is tightly structured. It has proven to be advantageous to ensure Six-Sigma practitioners are properly trained and skilled. Series of certifications start with basic practitioners (White Belts) running through Yellow Belt, Green Belt, Black Belt and Master Black Belt. It is simple enough to learn about the distinctions should you ever need to know.

LEAN Six-Sigma- As the name suggests, LEAN Six-Sigma is a combination of LEAN and Six-Sigma. The two approaches are complementary, so they mesh together well in theory. The evolution of methodologies and structures is on-going. The expected advantage of embracing the combined approach is to have a greater likelihood of finding and reducing waste and errors, thus contributing to the general goals of effectiveness and efficiency.

Concluding Thoughts About Quality

I offer five key points about quality (in the business sense).

First, define what quality means to your organization. Ensure your definition is measurable. As a corollary, measurements falling outside of tolerance limits should generate consequences or provoke action. If you ever see a quality system with lots of data and little reaction to data out of tolerance, then the system is probably flawed. In addition, the reactions should be significant. Putting a mark on a chart is not sufficient. In short, every measurable element in the definition of quality should be able to pass the "So what?" test.

Second, measure your present situation and changes in that situation.

Third, seek continuous improvement.

Fourth, embed quality into regular operations. Quality should not belong to another department or another manager. If it does, one risks creating a "we/they" situation that disconnects quality from other operations. At most, one might have a separate department to perform specialized tests, to measure incoming items, and to maintain certain records. Other than that, quality should be part of what we all do.

Fifth, quality systems are not magic. Any quality system can work. Any can fail. It is wise to pick a system that makes the best fit with the company, but it is vital to adapt the system to one's own operations and to embrace the system fully.

APPENDIX SECTION

Appendix A: Stockout Costs and Consequences

Angry customers or idle inventory?

(Originally published in 2008 by APICS Magazine)

APICS Editor's note: While operations management professionals can appreciate the tangible "inventory issues" associated with stockouts, many have considerable trouble understanding the related costs. APICS magazine Managing Editor Elizabeth Rennie recently spoke with John Van Vliet, Ph.D., an associate professor in the School of Business Management at Shorter College. Van Vliet is currently working to assign costs to potential stockouts and determine the pros and cons of contending with inventory carrying costs versus the risk of a stockout.

ELIZABETH RENNIE: Let's begin by talking about the challenges operations management professionals face when it comes to understanding the results associated with a stockout.

JOHN VAN VLIET: A stockout will generate a chain of costly events, and it's hard to assign costs to that chain and hard to know when to stop moving along the chain. For a manufacturer, a stockout can halt a production line or cause items to be set aside for rework. It can also create a rush of activity to find the needed item or material. Assigning a cost to that is challenging, and it kind of depends upon the situation. For a distributor, a stockout obviously generates the cost of processing and ultimately fulfilling a backorder. However, it also means a customer has been disappointed—and trying to assess the impact of the cost of that disappointment also is dependent upon the particular situation. Using a combination of financial data about a company's actual operations and a set of subjective judgments about immeasurable effects, we can take a stab at assigning a cost to a stockout. But we're never confident with that and, my goodness, it's astonishing how high that assigned cost can actually become.

RENNIE: Can you give me an example of something that did astonish you when you actually looked into how much a stockout was costing a company?

VAN VLIET: The worst case would be when a customer goes away—and assigning a cost to that is kind of easy: You just ask, "How much profit did we make on that customer over the past several years?" Well, you don't get that anymore. I had one customer who was very clever. He picked two electric parts distributors and gave us each a set of parts and said, "I will go to each one of you for the items on your list. As soon as you fail to provide me one of those items, I will move that item to the other guy's list. And, therefore, the cost of the stockout was we lost that customer's business for that particular item. I've also seen folks who've tried to assign cost values to production line stoppages, and those just go through the roof.

RENNIE: So we know that having a stockout absolutely changes customer demand in the future because they might not come back, first and foremost; or, at the very least, they might change their ordering habits.

VAN VLIET: Yes, that's painfully clear. And the sales team will beat you up about stockouts and make sure you know that customers get massively disappointed when we cause them problems. We're supposed to be making problems go away for them, not developing problems for them. And when you think about all of the time, money and effort we spend trying to attract customers, isn't it silly to say we're going to fine-tune our inventory controls and accept a higher degree of risk of disappointing our customers in order to save a few hundred dollars here and there?

Something else to consider: Sometimes, as inventory control specialists, we spend an awful lot of time looking at very, very small amounts of capital—low-volume items with low price tags. And maybe it's more rational to save a bunch of time by having extra of those items on hand because the amount of capital they consume is really petty small compared to the amount of time that we would spend managing little bitty items.

RENNIE: Looking at specific types of items, would you say A, B, or C items mean the worst-case scenario for a firm if they experience a stockout?

VAN VLIET: The definition of A, B, and C items is often associated with usage rates; so, actually, I think the better question to ask is, "Which items are the real showstoppers?" I'd rather take a look at which items will hurt us the worst. So, for a manufacturer, a fuse on a machine at a process bottleneck is a critical item. If that fuse blows, the process halts until the fault is corrected and the fuse is replaced. On the other hand, a fuse on a machine in a slack part of the process is less critical. So, if the operations team has properly categorized the inventory parts, we should be able to say to the purchasers, "Here are some items that we must not stock out of, so we will accept a very low rate of inventory turns on these items."

For a distributor, the question really hinges on expectations: What do the customers expect? For example, a customer would be astonished if a plumbing supply distributor ran out of half-inch copper couplings. The customer would be more understanding of a stockout of some sort of a specialized faucet.

What we promise the customer also matters enormously. When I was an operations manager for an electric parts distributor, the sales team had finally managed to win the business of a large original equipment manufacturer (OEM). As part of that agreement, we promised to be able to supply a certain number of specific parts to that OEM at any time. Obviously, a stockout of one of those items would've been a killer.

So, if the items can be properly categorized, then we can accept the higher risk of stockouts for less important items—maybe C items,—but we couldn't accept the stockout of something that we might call an A-plus item, and that's kind of where I'm going with the thought processes on how to decide which items we have to manage very closely in order to avoid a stockout.

RENNIE: And, in your opinion, you feel those are the inexpensive items, but that does not necessarily mean C items.

VAN VLIET: Well, keep in mind that some low-usage rate items, which are typically categorized as C, could actually turn out to be some of these highly critical items. So, as with the example with that OEM that we had finally managed to land, some of the items that OEM cared about were not particularly critical items to us. They were obviously C items. But because of the promise to that OEM, I kicked them up into the A-plus category.

RENNIE: So a customer can view an item in one way, and you can certainly see it as something else. But really it's all about how the customer views it, and you just have to respond to that.

VAN VLIET: The customer's view is really significant. I have a great example of that: My company sold Rockwell Automation equipment, and that equipment uses a set of specialized heater elements. We were the only source of the heater elements in the area. The sales manager came to me and said, "Hey, John, we're gonna drive customers away from us and from that product line if we ever stock out of these heater elements. We should have plenty of them on time all the time, but we've been stocking out." He was exactly right. All I had to do was to adjust the order controls on those heater elements by adding safety stock so the reorder points were exceptionally high. I wanted us to have nine months of usage or more on hand for every single variety of those heater elements. Given that they were inexpensive, it was easy to do. Given that the price of these heater elements was low and the amount of money we would have to stack on our shelves in heater elements would be relatively small, it was easy for me to make an arbitrary judgment and lift the order point controls.

When we look at an item and try to figure out if we have to take Herculean efforts to make sure we don't stock out of the item, one of the things we also want to look at is how responsive is the rest of the supply chain to that item. Suppose we say to a customer, "You give us an order, and tomorrow we're delivering the item," but later we get an order and discover we are out in a stockout situation. If it's relatively easy to get that item in time, well then, stocking out would not be quite a disaster. It would cause us the aggravation of jumping around and solving the problem, but we would be able to break the chain of bad consequences if we could get that part and still get it to the customer in time.

So, a highly responsible supply chain behind us minimizes the amount of fear we have of a stockout. This means that, when we're assessing a particular item and trying to decide what our reorder point ought to be for the item, the responsiveness of the supply chain really does come into play.

RENNIE: After everything we discussed, now, how does a person go about striking the right balance between keeping inventory on hand and risking a stockout?

VAN VLIET: Actually, I'm quite fascinated by this question. Right now, what we tend to do is measure stockout rates and fuss at the purchasers when those stockout rates are too high. Of course, at the same time, we measure inventory turns and fuss at the purchasers when the turns are too low. We've figured out how to help purchasers do a better job deciding how much to order by giving them formulas such as economic order quantities. But perhaps we need some kind of a similar formula—one that includes a factor for the cost of stockouts—that could help us determine the best order points. It's obviously the order point, not the order quantity, that is the biggest factor in determining whether we're going to face a stockout or not.

The advice I would give our fellow professionals is to do two things: The first thing, the thing I did that tended to work, is to rank order the active inventory by the dollar value of the items in the stock. When you do that, you can then establish a cut-off line and say, "We have $ 10 Million worth of inventory, but below this line is maybe half of our inventory items, and it only amounts to $900,000. Well, all the items below that cut-off line really consume only a fraction of the capital we have devoted to inventory, but each item is a stockout risk, and a customer can be just as disappointed if you stock out of an inexpensive item as an expensive one. Customers care about getting their item or not. So, if you take the set of items below the cut-off line and increase the order points on those items, you've added just a little bit more inventory that you're carrying in terms of pure inventory capital, but you bought enormous stockout insurance for the mass of items below the line.

The second thing inventory managers should do is identify the showstoppers. These are the A-plus items, the ones where the stockout would really be horrible, and they have to increase the reorder points for those items. Now, I don't quite know how to do that. I have done it before in an arbitrary way, and then I ran the numbers and figured out how much additional capital would be added to our inventory and choked. I said, "Oh, that's no good." But then you go to the biggest culprits—the ones that carry the largest chunk of extra capital—and look at them to see if there's some sort of a way to minimize the risk of a stockout or the consequences.

Another approach I took was to go to a customer who wanted us to have a certain number of parts—and some of these were quite expensive—and I said, "Well, based on your usage rates, you're asking me to stock a heck of a lot of stuff that you don't really need. Couldn't we agree on a

different level? Or could we agree that you stock some of it?"
And so we began to negotiate on how to handle the large
chunk of capital the customer was asking us to stash on our
shelves.

Finally, what I'm working on right now is trying to figure out
some way to incorporate a proper cost of stockout into the
reorder point factor; but I'm just not there yet.

Key Quote:

"A customer can be just as disappointed if you stock out of
an inexpensive item as an expensive one."

From APICS Magazine 2008

Appendix B: Inventory Management – Real Benefits from a Focus on Returns

(Manuscript of "Dead Stock", APICS Extra, Vol. 2, No. 10, October 31, 2007)

John H. Van Vliet III, Ph.D.

Inventory management is a significant element in the study of Operations Management. Much of the analytical effort in this area has centered on developing useful ordering controls, but other factors are also important to the study of inventory management. This article adds to the study of inventory management by considering the costly problem of inactive inventory and by offering the suggestion that companies can benefit by paying formal attention to inventory return activities. The article opens with a brief presentation of the efforts to improve inventory management through improved ordering mechanisms. It then introduces the problem of inactive or "dead" stock. The magnitude of the problem of inactive stock is illustrated with evidence from several companies. The article then presents comparative evidence of the beneficial impact of including a formal mechanism to return inactive stock to suppliers within agreed time frames.

Focus on Ordering Controls

Recognizing that stocks of inventory represent a substantial amount of money to many companies, and recognizing that inventory shortfalls (stockouts) can seriously disrupt operations, inventory managers seek to create inventory management activities and procedures that are both efficient and effective. Efficient inventory management will productively use the financial assets committed to inventory stocks. Effective inventory management will satisfy the needs of internal or external customers by avoiding stock outs. Much of the work in the area of inventory management has sought to achieve efficient and effective inventory levels by focusing on the communication of requirements for items and on the development of effective ordering controls for those items.

Numerous ordering control techniques are offered by experts and by firms providing inventory management systems. For example, NxTrend Technology uses the following "six order methods: min/max, product classification, economic order quantity (EOQ), human, blanket order, and quantity break."(Buyer, 2002, p. 28) These control methods share the common goal of deciding how much of an item to purchase and when to make that purchase. A variety of factors and assumptions characterize each method, and no single method seems to suit all circumstances.

For the most part, these methods and their variants share some common elements. They use an "available stock on hand" level to trigger the need to replenish an item. This level can be fixed or it can change based on usage rates. Then they use various mechanisms to determine how much to purchase. This purchase quantity can be a fixed quantity, a quantity based on usage or cost, or, in the case of EOQ, a quantity based on the costs of ordering and the costs of maintaining inventory.

EOQ is particularly interesting because it is the only common mechanism to use both the cost of the item and the cost of keeping the item on the shelves. EOQ uses the following formula to calculate how much of an item to purchase:

$$\text{Order Quantity} = \sqrt{\frac{24 * \text{Monthly Usage} * \text{Cost of Ordering}}{\text{Carrying Cost \%} * \text{Cost of Item}}}$$

The "carrying cost" is a factor intended to account for the costs of having an item in inventory. It is expressed as a percentage of the value of the item and accounts for the cost of capital locked into the item, the cost of warehouse space needed for the item, the cost of insurance for the item, the cost for activities associated with the item (such as counting it), and the risk that the item will become obsolete. One survey found that the carrying cost factor may range from 18% to 42% (Schreibfeder). However, although EOQ does consider the carrying cost, it is important to remember that EOQ is intended only to determine the quantity to be purchased. It has no purpose related to removing inactive stock or dead stock.

What happens after the purchasers are finished and the items are on the shelves? If the demand forecast was accurate, then the items will be sold over time and new stock will be purchased to replenish them. However, if the forecast was wrong on the optimistic side, then the items will move off the shelves only slowly or not at all. This creates the entirely separate problem of sluggish, inactive or dead stock in the warehouse.

Dead Stock

Dead stock is a double loss. The money used to purchase the stock in the first place is consumed. On top of that, maintaining dead stock in a warehouse involves annual "carrying" costs to count, store and insure the items. Financial logic indicates a company should rid itself of the dead stock and avoid the carrying costs even if the dead stock must be totally written off.

The magnitude of the problem of dead stock will vary from company to company. Some companies may be disciplined in writing off dead stock and may, accordingly, carry inventories with a relatively small percentage of dead stock. Other companies may be more reluctant to write off the dead stock and may carry a larger percentage of dead stock. In an effort to understand the magnitude of the problem of dead stock, the author studied the inventory of five companies in the distribution industry. In each company, the study measured the dollar volume of the inventory on hand, the dollar volume of inventory that had been inactive for greater than 6 months, and the dollar volume of inventory that had been inactive for greater than 12 months. (An inactive item is one that has not been sold, transferred or purchased

within the time frame.) The results are shown in figure 1
below as percentages of the total inventory.

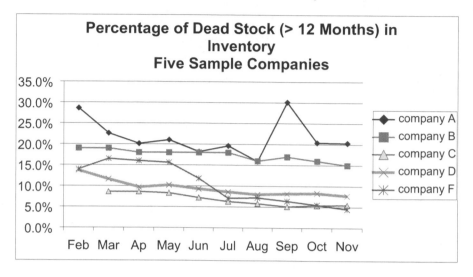

Figure 1.

The figure shows that these companies carry substantial
amounts of dead stock. The amounts range from a low of
about 5% to a high of greater than 20%. (The September
figure of 30% for Company A seems to be non-
representative.) Company C tends to report the lowest
percentage of dead stock, and, as one would expect,
managers at Company C state they systematically review
dead stock for write off. Company A reports the highest
percentage of dead stock and, as one would also expect,
rarely writes of stock that has not moved. In all cases,
however, the amount of capital tied up in dead stock is
substantial.

Obviously, writing off dead stock is an expensive process.
One naturally wonders if there isn't something to be done to
minimize the loss. Accepting that sales forecasts cannot be
perfect and that ordering algorithms cannot be perfect either,

it seems inevitable that a company will purchase some stock that it cannot use. Is this stock destined to become dead and written off, or is there something else to be done? Given that many suppliers will accept returns of stock under certain conditions, might that not be a path forward?

The premise of this article is that a formal method of managing inventory, with an emphasis on returning stock before it must be written off, will reduce dead stock substantially, without having to write it off, and result in cost savings that are greater than the cost of tracking the potentially dead stock.

One can imagine a purchasing manager being converted into a "return manager". In many organizations, purchasing algorithms supported by data from the organization's information system generate purchase orders that may or may not be reviewed by human purchasing managers. Suppose the purchasing manager were to build a gross filter to catch major errors in the system, (For instance, only show orders with a value in excess of $5,000.) The filter would catch major errors and permit other purchases to be processed automatically. This would free time for the purchasing manager to focus attention on inventory that is not moving well. The task of the manager would be to identify stock that can be returned before it exceeds expiration dates or agreed return time limits.

Would such a shift in attention produce valuable results? Happily, there is a way to subject the idea to an empirical test without having to take the risk of introducing changes to ongoing practices. This technique relies on the fact that Panduit, a supplier of electrical parts, provides a vendor management service with a heavy focus on returning to Panduit stock that is not moving. (It is important to note that

Panduit's vendor managed inventory process did not reduce dead stock by writing it off.)   A company that has agreed to have Panduit manage its inventory becomes a laboratory to evaluate the impact of "purchasing business as usual" against a program that includes an emphasis on returns.

The Method: The author took inventory data from a company that carried the Panduit line and had agreed to allow Panduit to manage the stock levels of Panduit items. The data was sorted to identify items that had not had any activity in the last 12 months and parts that had not had any activity in the last 6 to 12 months. This provided three categories of parts in inventory. The first category would be parts that are considered "dead"; they have not moved in 12 months.   The second category consisted of parts that are inactive as they have not moved in 6 to 12 months. The third category is normal active inventory. The data was then sorted by manufacturer in order to compare the levels of Panduit parts against the levels of all other items.

The Results: The results are shown in Figure 2. Rounding to the nearest thousand, one sees the company carried $123,000 of Panduit inventory. $7,000 (5.5%) of that was inactive and $9,000 (7.1%) was dead. Total Panduit inventory that had not moved in 6 months or more represented 12.6% of the total value of Panduit inventory. For all items other than Panduit, the corresponding figures were $2,885,000 of inventory value, of which $216,000 (7.5%) was inactive and $339,000 (11.8%) was dead. Total inventory that had not moved in 6 months or more represented 19.2% of the total value of inventory other than Panduit.

	Panduit	%	All Other Inventory (Less Panduit)	%	Applying Panduit % to All Other	Savings
Total Inventory	$123,000		$2,885,000			
Inactive Stock (> 6 but < 12 mos)	$7,000	5.5 %	$216,000	7.5 %	$159,000	$57,000
Dead Stock (> 12 mos)	$9,000	7.1 %	$339,000	11.8 %	$205,000	$134,000
					Total Savings	$191,000

Figure 2 – Shows savings from potential reduction in non-performing inventory

Analysis: What would the situation look like if the purchasing manager could cause the entire inventory to match Panduit's percentage of inactive or dead stock? Inactive stock would drop from $223,000 to $164,000. Dead stock would drop from $348,000 to $214,000. A total of $191,000 (6.4%) of inactive or dead inventory would be avoided. This particular company assigns a carry cost of 35% to its inventory, so the reduction of $191,000 in inventory represents an annual savings of $67,000 in addition to the major benefit of using the $191,000 to purchase useful inventory rather than having to write it off.

Certainly, not all companies will have dead stock percentages similar to those of the company used for this analysis. Nor is there any guarantee that all companies could achieve similar savings. However, the evidence in this case shows the attractiveness of controlling dead stock levels through returns rather than write-offs.

Conclusion: In the quest to improve the efficiency and effectiveness of inventory, purchasers presently concentrate on finding improved methods to determine when to order stock and how much to order. The limited evidence examined by the author strongly suggests that purchasers can make a substantial future contribution to the bottom line of their companies by focusing attention on returning items before they become inactive or dead.

References

Buyer Guide NxTrend (2002). NxTrend Technology, Inc. Colorado Springs, CO   Printed in U.S.A July 2002

Schreibfeder, J. (2000) How Much Does It Cost You To Buy? Published on the Internet by Effective Inventory Management, Coppel, Texas. Retrieved on August 24th, 2007 from http://www.effectiveinventory.com/article38.html

Summary

- Purchasers should become "return managers".
- Focus on returns to avoid dead stock.
- Smarter "returning" has a big payoff.

Appendix C: Economic Order Quantity - Values for Ordering and Holding Costs

 EOQ (Economic Order Quantity) is one of the tools managers use to find the optimal size of an order that balances the cost of ordering against the cost of holding inventory. The ordering cost, C, represents the time and other expenses associated with developing and placing an order and then receiving the shipment. The inventory holding cost, H, represents the costs of keeping inventory in the warehouse; costs such as interest, insurance, wastage, loss, counting, etc.

The optimal order quantity is determined by the following formula (where U is the usage rate):

EOQ = SQRT (2*U*C/H)

Obviously, selecting the right values for C (Ordering cost) and H (Holding cost) is important to managers who want to use EOQ.   In the last half of 2011, 117 APICS members participated in a survey to determine what their companies use as values for Ordering Costs and for Holding Costs.

This is a report of the results:

Cost of Ordering: The results were highly mixed. Some responses were subjective and had to be excluded. Some were obvious errors, such as the $7,000,000 reply or the replies that reported percentages. 64 responses were between one dollar and $500. The average was $87. 45% of those answers were between $25 and $99. 28% were between $100 and $199.

 Conclusion for Ordering Cost: Particularly low values for C suggest the inventory managers are not considering the costs associated with receiving. The scattered nature of the values between $25 and $199 suggests either substantial variation among business activities or inventory managers are just guessing about values for C. An ordering cost value between $25 and $200 is common.

 Holding Costs: Again, the results were highly mixed. (Part of that could be due to exceptionally high holding costs associated with perishable products.) 68 responses were between one percent and fifty percent. 21% of the answers were under ten percent. 72% were between ten percent and thirty percent. The average was of the responses was eighteen percent.

Conclusion for Holding Costs: Holding costs include cost of capital, tax costs, counting or maintenance costs, and wastage, among other things. Except for cost of capital and taxes, the nature of the items in inventory can skew the costs. If your company uses a Holding cost near 18%, you are typical. If your value is substantially different, you might want to examine the elements of the holding cost you use to ensure you are satisfied with it.

General conclusion and comment: The odd responses and the highly varied responses suggest there may be confusion about how to use EOQ. The goal of EOQ is to help companies efficiently determine order quantities by balancing ordering costs against holding costs. If the values used for C and H are wobbly, then the utility of using EOQ becomes suspect.

John Van Vliet, Ph.D.
Department of Business and Public Policy
Young Harris College
2012

ABOUT THE AUTHOR, JOHN H. VAN VLIET III

John spent his youth as an Army brat and then followed in his father's footsteps by serving 24 years in the US Army as an Infantry Officer. He is proud to claim the 75th Ranger Regiment as his regiment. John retired as a Lieutenant Colonel in 1994.

John began a second career in the distribution and automation engineering industry. He was Operations Manager for a $30 million electric parts distributor in Greenville, SC. He then became the Director of a $160 million business unit with 13 locations in three states.

John retired from the distribution and automation engineering industry after seven years in order to earn his Doctorate and focus on teaching. He is now the Professor of Business and Public Policy at YHC

John is married to his high school sweetheart. They live in Hiawassee, Georgia and have two grown daughters plus three grandsons.

Education:
- Capella University –   2005   Ph.D. Operations and Management
- Georgia State University - 1978   MBA
- Georgetown University   - 1973   MA Political Science
- U. S. Military Academy-   1970   BS Engineering
- French War College, Paris, France_ - 1988

Teaching Experience:

- Professor, Department of Business and Public Policy, Young Harris College, (2008 - Present)
- Cohort Professor, Norwich University MBA program, (2002 - 2015)
- Assistant Professor, Shorter College, (Management) (2005 – 2008)
- Assistant Professor, U.S. Military Academy, (Economics, Political Philosophy) (1979-1983)
- Instructor, Masters Program, Boston University, London UK (Management) (1992-1993)
- Lecturer, Ministry of Defense, London UK (National Security Policy) (1992-1994)
- Adjunct Faculty, Georgia Perimeter College (Government), (2001-2002)

Made in the USA
Columbia, SC
01 November 2022

70297115R00067